Life as a Casketeer

Life as a Casketeer

Francis & Kaiora Tipene

with Paul Little

HarperCollins_Publishers_

Ka mihi ki a Stephanie Huirana Fong rāua ko
Julian Wilcox mō te taha whakataukī.

HarperCollins*Publishers*

First published in 2020
by HarperCollins*Publishers* (New Zealand) Limited
Unit D1, 63 Apollo Drive, Rosedale, Auckland 0632, New Zealand
harpercollins.co.nz

HarperCollins*Publishers*
Unit D1, 63 Apollo Drive, Rosedale, Auckland 0632, New Zealand
Level 13, 201 Elizabeth Street, Sydney NSW 2000, Australia
A 53, Sector 57, Noida, UP, India
1 London Bridge Street, London, SE1 9GF, United Kingdom
Bay Adelaide Centre, East Tower, 22 Adelaide Street West, 41st floor,
   Toronto, Ontario M5H 4E3, Canada
195 Broadway, New York NY 10007, USA

A catalogue record for this book is available from the National Library of New Zealand

ISBN 978 1 7755 4148 6 (paperback)
ISBN 978 1 7754 9179 8 (ebook)
ISBN 978 1 4607 8141 8 (audio book)

Cover design by Amy Daoud, HarperCollins Design Studio
Front cover photo by Lottie Hedley
All images on the back cover and in the picture section are from the Tipene family collection
Typeset in Minion Pro by Kirby Jones
Printed and bound in Australia by McPherson's Printing Group
The papers used by HarperCollins in the manufacture of this book are a natural, recyclable
product made from wood grown in sustainable plantation forests. The fibre source and
manufacturing processes meet recognised international environmental standards, and carry
certification.

This book is dedicated to
Walter and Helen Tipene
and Hani and Ruana Murray

Ki te kore koutu mei kore hoki ko māua

_____

If it weren't for you, we wouldn't be here

WAIATA TANGI

Rimurimu, tere tere
E rere ki te moana.
E tere ana ki te ripo
I waho e.

Seaweed drifting, drifting,
floating on the ocean.
Drifting in the whirlpool,
out there.

Tirohia i waho rā
E marino ana e.
Kei roto i ahau
E marangai ana e.

When I look out there
it is so calm.
While within me
everything is storm-tossed.

Kei te tio te huka
I runga o ngā hiwi.
Kei te moe koromeke
Te wairua e.

The snow is biting cold
on the ridges.
And lying curled up asleep
is your spirit.

Rite tonu tō hanga
Ki te tīrairaka e
Waihoki tō hanga
Te wairangi e.

Your behaviour is like that
of the fantail,
in the same way, your restless spirit
upsets me greatly.

PEPEHA

FRANCIS

Ko Makora te maunga
Ko Rotokākahi te awa
Ko Whangapē te moana
Ko Taiao te marae
Ko Ngātokimatawhaorua te waka

KAIORA

Ko Te Rangi Āniwaniwa te maunga
Ko Rangaunu te moana
Ko Pūwheke te maunga
Ko Waimanoni te marae
Ko Māmari te waka

CONTENTS

Ko te tai tamatāne,
ko te tai i whakatūria e Kupe ki te marowhara

———————————

The western sea,
stirred up by Kupe at the casting off of his war belt

CHAPTER ONE

YOUNG FRANCIS

A LOT OF PEOPLE know me as that funeral director from TV. But when I was growing up, we didn't have a TV. Or the electricity to run one. Or a toilet. Or indoor running water.

Although I was born in 1983, I spent my first few years living like it was a century earlier.

I was raised in Pawarenga in Northland, mainly by my grandparents Walter and Helen Tipene, and I'm so glad I was. It was an upbringing like very few people have these days. Everything we did was done the hard way, and it has meant I appreciate every single thing I have now.

Pawarenga is on the west coast of the Far North and very isolated. Its official population is … not many. But my family's roots there go back a long way. The closest 'big town' is Kaitaia, which is sixty-three kilometres away. It's not very close. It's not very big, either.

But that's not where I started life. That was further south, in Auckland at St Helen's Hospital. My mother, Helen Tipene, is Māori, and my father, Francis Muller, is of Tongan descent.

They were two young sweethearts – much too young as far as my mum's mother was concerned. Dad was twenty and Mum was just eighteen. When I arrived, my grandmother swooped down from Northland and told her daughter how it was going to be.

'You can't take care of a baby at your age,' said Nan. 'Give him to us and we will look after him.'

Nan was and is our family matriarch and the biggest single influence on my life. She is very traditional in all things, a great upholder of tikanga, and the person we always run things past when we're not sure. To this day, I might think I can get away with something, but suddenly Nan is there shaking her head: 'No, no, no, no.' I love that she always does that. She keeps me grounded and stops my head getting too big.

And so I was handed over to my grandparents and taken north. I was a whāngai kid – a pretty common practice used by Māori families to make sure their children are brought up okay. Which I was.

Thanks to my being in that TV show, a lot of people know a bit about me – but they often only know half the story. For instance, a lot of Tongan people who come in to arrange funerals know I'm half Tongan, on my father's side, and they ask why I am a Tipene not a Muller, so I have to explain to them about my Māori family and the whāngai system.

I was given my Māori whānau surname at birth. It's on my birth certificate. Mum did the paperwork, although I think the name might have been my grandmother's idea. Whatever the reason, it was obviously out of my hands.

*

IT CAN'T HAVE BEEN EASY for Nan and Pop to take on a baby at their age. Although they would have been in their fifties, and that is young to be a grandparent these days, they had already started on a new life of their own.

Up until not long before I was born, they had been living in Auckland. Nan worked mainly as a dry-cleaner and Pop worked for the Power Board, but they sold their house and moved north to settle on our family land and build their house there. It was a very frugal life and money was short, which is why we went without so many things that other people take for granted.

Pop was a hardworking man who liked to stay in the background. We are quite different. Somehow, I have grown up comfortable with an audience and talking to big groups of people. Pop would never have done that. He was a quiet person, who didn't want to be any trouble to anyone. He would never ask for help with things, so when I was older, we had to work out what our grandparents needed and just go ahead and do it for them.

It was a simple existence. We had a cow for our milk – Pop took care of that. And there was a bore at the top of the hill for our fresh water. So we had nearly everything we needed to make a cup of tea, apart from boiling the water.

For that, we had gas tanks. But we still had to be careful how much we used. At bath time I went first, then Nan, then Pop. That was fine then, but as I've gotten older and looked back I feel a little differently about it. Fortunately, kids don't think like that, and I didn't mind at the time.

Thursday was benefit day, when we went to Kaitaia to do our shopping. We filled up the gas bottles and got kerosene so we'd have light and heat at home. All I ever wanted was a pie and an ice cream. And maybe a Hubba Bubba bubble gum. That was Nan and Pop's treat – so simple, but I loved it and have never lost my taste for pies and ice cream.

For an extra special treat, we had a SodaStream machine at home. Regular fizzy drinks were too expensive, but the SodaStream brought much happiness to us all.

Nan and Pop were very religious. Pawarenga has a beautiful old church called St Gabriel's that stands on a hill overlooking the harbour. We went to church a lot. It was my grandmother's hope that I would become a Catholic priest. That didn't happen. Quite the opposite, in fact, although I do spend a lot of time in churches now.

I didn't need to go to St Gabriel's for my church experience. To this day, the inside of Nan's house is like a church itself, with pictures of Mary everywhere you look. Nan loves Mary.

We weren't one of those families that had regular prayers night and morning, but we did say grace, though not out loud. Pop took his hat off and made the sign of the cross, praying quietly to himself, and then he started eating. When we weren't eating at home, Pop lifted his hat briefly then put it back on before a meal.

Because Pawarenga is very remote, the only other kids were a long way away, so I was pretty isolated from people my own age. I grew up to be a bit of a loner and different from other kids, because I had no one to copy.

I had to entertain myself – and so did Nan and Pop. They played cards a lot, read magazines and did crosswords.

There was plenty of wide open space for me to play in. I liked being outdoors when I was allowed to be, but Nan was quite protective: 'Don't go out there … It's too cold … You'll get dirty.'

I was handed over to my grandparents and taken north. I was a whāngai kid – a pretty common practice used by Māori families to make sure their children are brought up okay.

Actually, we did have a TV – sort of, sometimes. It was a tiny old black and white set, and every so often Pop got the battery out of the car and hooked it up so we could watch *Sale of the Century*.

The prizes and the lights and the noise – it was all so different from anything in my own life it had me completely spellbound. In fact, all three of us were glued to the set. I even loved the black and white dots that crackled away while it was warming up.

Pop was very clever like that. He could fix just about anything and nothing was officially broken in our house until he couldn't fix it one more time.

Even though Pop had worked for the Power Board, my grandparents only got the power on at Pawarenga about five years ago, and they never got completely used to it. At night, if they went to the toilet, they used a torch instead of turning on the light, and Nan still does. She is very stuck in her ways, and I love her for it.

A lot of people find it hard to believe that life could be like that for a family in the 1980s but it was. And we weren't the only ones. At the time this was happening, my future wife's family and her brothers and sisters were having a similar upbringing over on the east coast.

Later, when I was at Hato Petera College in Auckland with other Māori kids, and they talked about how they had been brought up, we found we were all very similar. So I knew there were different ways of life, but I always felt the way I was brought up was quite normal.

It's a good way to be raised, because you learn to be self-reliant. And when you don't know what you're missing, you don't mind that you don't have a lot of toys and gadgets. I suppose that's true, but I would have liked a few more toys.

I didn't have a lot to do with my father as a child, but had regular contact with my mother, when Nan and Pop would take me on the five-hour drive to Auckland to see her. I loved it. It was such a contrast to Pawarenga that it was like going on holiday overseas.

Coming into Auckland over the Harbour Bridge and seeing that huge city with all its tall buildings spread out and with the lights on at night was amazing. Mum lived in a regular state house in Glen Eden, but it was as good as Disneyland to me. I was fascinated by the electric lighting, and spent ages just flicking the switch on and off. And not only that – Mum had a tap you could turn to make water come out, and a toilet you could flush.

She also had a key to the swimming pool at the local school, which was great. The creek at Pawarenga was great too, but the pool in Auckland was something else.

It was all so simple. Going to the pools and having fish and chips afterwards was massive. I also loved driving anywhere in the car and going into the centre of town at night to see all the bright lights.

Back up north, if I got $20 for my birthday or managed to earn it somehow, I never wanted to spend it. I wanted to look at it and love it and hold onto it until I got to the city.

Around that time, the two-dollar shops were just coming in, and they were heaven to me. You could get so much for $2. So, when I was ready to part with the $20 bill I had obsessed over for so long, that was where I went.

It was hard seeing my mum in that off-and-on way because I was always so happy to get there and then so sad when we had to leave. I knew she was my mum and I knew she loved me and I did miss her when we were apart. When it was time to go, I cried and cried. I wanted to stay with her in the house where you could turn the lights on and off.

Nan was the strong one: 'No. You've got to come home.' She and my mother would have fights about it.

'There's nothing up there for him,' said my mother, which was partly true.

'You can't even look after him,' said my grandmother, which was also true.

I wasn't happy, sitting in the back of the car as we headed back north.

'Mum said there's nothing up there for me,' I complained once. 'Why do I have to come back?'

'You're coming.'

Looking back at it now, I wouldn't have had it any other way. I'm so thankful, although at the time I was angry at Nan and sad for Mum. I'm thankful to Mum for wanting me and to Nan for taking me. And they both know that's how I feel.

Mum did manage to get up north for a visit too from time to time. I know she brought up the idea of me going back to live with her, but Nan was adamant. There might have been an argument, but Mum wouldn't have got very far in an argument with Nan.

I don't hold it against either of them. I love them both equally, but I'm grateful my mother let me go with Nan. I love her even more now for doing that.

I'm not sure what life would have been like if I had stayed in Auckland. I might not have got the same foundation and start in life if Nan hadn't looked after me. I know it hurt me and my mother, but looking back, I think that was a beautiful hurt.

Certainly, there were some sad times there, but I think it was good to learn about being sad. That has come in handy now that I help others in their sad times. And I learnt how to get by and deal with life's happenings, even if they weren't things I would have chosen to happen.

My mum stayed single for a while, then she met Raymond, who was Samoan, and they had Moana and Peta, my sisters, who I also looked forward to spending time with on my Auckland visits. We never say 'step' or 'half' in our family – we are just brother and sisters.

Unfortunately, Raymond died young in a house fire. Mum stayed single again for a long time and my sisters grew up in Auckland without a dad. Mum did a great job with them. They are two beautiful human beings who I also missed when I went back to Pawarenga after my visits. Later, my mother met Peter and they have been together for several years. He had children from before too, so ours is a great big mix-up of a family. I've watched TV programmes about step-parenting and how it works or doesn't. Our family works, but I'm not sure why. I just know that when we come together, we are all really good friends with lots of shared experiences to remember.

It all adds to everything I am. I'm glad about the different ways we've been brought up in our family, because it's happening to more and more people these days and I come across a lot of it in my funeral work: there are step-families, half-siblings, multiple wives and husbands. There can be so many different dynamics that a funeral director needs to take into account and it's easier when I can work from my own experience.

*

IN MANY THINGS, Nan was easy-going and open-minded. She wasn't big on rules, but when it came to church and things at the marae, tangihanga and unveilings, her line was: 'This is the way we do things.' There would be no deviating.

She wasn't just religious, she was also very superstitious and held on to a lot of traditional Māori beliefs. All put together, that was a powerful combination and I've absorbed a lot of it.

Around the time my grandfather died, I had a beautiful photo of him in my home in Auckland. The house is open plan with the kitchen, dining area and lounge all together.

'When I walk into my house, I want to see Pop right there over by the table,' I told Nan.

'No. He can't be looking at you while you're eating,' she said. 'Put him around the other side so he's facing the TV.'

And that was because in Māori culture, food is noa, or profane, and has to be kept away from death, which is tapu, or sacred – and for Nan, that difference extended to photos of dead people as well.

She was big on prayer too, with lots of little karakia for different things. She still gives a lot of time to the church at Pawarenga. She is always up there cleaning. For people in the country, the church is a place to be together as a community, not just on Sundays but any time they can go there to do something useful.

When Nan comes to my funeral home in town, she always has a good look around. If she says, 'This is a nice cross,' I know that means she thinks it would be perfect in St Gabriel's Church. Or she might ask for leftover decorations that have been used on a casket, or any ornaments of Mary or Jesus that are spare. I know it will make her happy to take them, so I'm happy to give them to her.

My grandfather was also devout but a lot quieter about not

just that but most other things. For instance, after they got the phone put on, he would never answer it if he could avoid it. You would always get Nan on the other end if you rang up.

If she wasn't there, and you hung on long enough, he would pick it up, but it was torture for him with his long drawn out 'Hellooooo' after a pause and lots more pauses after that. He was a shy man and by that time he was not well. But he knew he had to answer the phone because it might have been Nan and he would have been in big trouble if he didn't pick up.

MY PATERNAL GREAT-GRANDMOTHER – Pop's mother – is another important personality in the background of my story, although I never met her. She was a big woman and went by her nickname, Nana Wissy, although her real name was Nana Raiha.

She was also a devout Catholic who brought up Pop and his fourteen brothers and sisters to be strong in their faith. I know she hoped one of the tamariki would become a priest or a nun, but that didn't happen. There was a lot of praying about that. But a generation later, one of her mokopuna did – my uncle Peter Tipene is a Catholic priest. In 2017, he was made dean of St Patrick's Cathedral in Auckland, and Nana Wissy would have been so proud of that. I'm sure she's up above, smiling and happy about it right now.

We still don't have a nun in the family, though. And I haven't done anything to help the cause with my six sons.

Pop and my family don't talk about Nana Wissy much, but because she was a larger-than-life character, other people do. Often when I go to a new marae and I tell people my name and where I am from, they say: 'Oh, was your grandma Wissy?'

She wasn't just religious, she was also very superstitious and held on to a lot of traditional Māori beliefs. All put together, that was a powerful combination and I've absorbed a lot of it.

And then they start telling me all about her. She was apparently famous for saying 'God bless you' to people in response to just about anything they said. She was a big influence in the Catholic Māori community, both in Auckland and up north.

It's humbling and beautiful to see how respected she was and I regret not talking to Pop about her more before he died in 2018. Sadly, he wasn't one for talking much about himself or his upbringing. I have good reason to know how important it is to do things while people are alive because you never know when they may be taken.

Even as a child, like all Māori kids but especially those living in the country, I learnt about tangi. And along with that, I learnt a lot about marae life and Māori funeral traditions.

Tangi were part of daily life. One moment you were outside playing with your friends and whānau and the next you heard the car horns start tooting from about a kilometre away. That was the signal to the home people that the manuhiri were nearly there. It was an eerie feeling. Once you knew what was going on and what the sound of the horns ringing down the valley of Pawarenga meant, you almost started to cry automatically. Even today when I take bodies up north from Auckland, as we draw near home we start tooting.

It was definitely the signal for us kids to stop what we were doing. We were ordered to get inside the wharenui. The cooks took off their aprons and came out of the kitchen along with everyone else, taking their places to receive the body. We had the pōwhiri and the karanga and we knew that whoever the person was, he or she was coming home for the last time.

When a mate, or dead body, was coming onto the marae and Nan was there, her cries were so sad. If Nan cried, it was so heart-rending and you cried too. You couldn't help yourself as she wailed and carried on. I knew why she was crying, but the fact that it was her made it even more painful. As she made her lament, I looked at her, thinking: *This is a side of someone you don't see often and, when you do, it opens up another realm of life.* All I knew of Nan was her happily putting me in my place, the matriarch of our home.

IN THE PAST few years I have probably seen more of my father than I did when I was growing up, and that's made me very happy. It's easier for us to be together now.

My dad was also in Auckland when I was a child. He had moved on and had a family of his own with my step-mum, Debbie. He worked at Lion Breweries in East Tamaki and has done since I was born. When we went to see my mum, I could also see my Tongan family – my dad and grandmother.

There was sadness in those visits too, because whenever I left that grandmother, she would be the one who cried.

When I was little, I think I was very different from the sort of boy Dad wanted, which was the boy who plays sport and is hands on with everything – someone who loves cars and making things. I love cars but they are very different from the kinds of car he's into.

Being so far away from him didn't help. And when Nan and Pop brought me to Auckland, it was mainly to see Mum, and so he had to fit in around that as well as his new family.

I saw a bit more of him when I lived with my Tongan grandmother for a while. We tried that when I was about six years old, but it didn't work because I missed Nan too much. I was used to being with her. I would ring her collect and cry down the phone about how much I missed her, every chance I got. It wasn't my Tongan grandmother's fault and I hope she knew I still loved her too.

Even this isn't all of the people who filled in as my parents when I was growing up. In the mid-nineties, I spent a lot of time, off and on, with my mother's sister and her husband – Aunty Bronwyn and Uncle George Proctor – at Pawarenga. They were dairy farmers and they had power and hot water, which was amazing. When I wasn't at Nan and Pop's, I was with them.

At that time, I went to the nearest convent school but I learnt just as much on the farm outside school hours as I did sitting in class. For a start, when I first went to my aunty and uncle's, I couldn't stand to get my hands dirty like a normal farm kid.

I learnt a few of the hard but necessary things you need to equip you for life. For instance, I learnt to be punctual, because it was a dairy farm, which meant that every morning, no matter how cold or rainy it was, you had to get up very early to do the milking. It wasn't optional. It had to happen, no matter how you felt.

I was about nine years old and it was a great experience, even though I didn't always think so at the time. Hindsight is very useful for making you feel better about things.

My cousin Darcy and I woke up – or Aunty knocked on the wall to wake us up – and then we would drag on our clothes and gumboots, get on the motorbike and call the dogs. Nowadays, you have to wear helmets and have roll bars, but back then there was none of that and there were no problems.

I loved working with the dogs. I knew all the whistles for the different commands they had to follow. I told my children about this recently and they didn't believe me, so I decided I'd have to brush up. The other night I was in the shower practising and my wife knocked on the door and wanted to know what I was doing, because it sure didn't sound like any song she knew. I explained I was trying to remember the dog whistles from the old days. She thought that was a bit strange, but she's used to that.

Darcy and I would round up the cows and take them to the shed, then herd them back to whichever paddock they needed to be in that day, close the gate and leave them to get ready for the afternoon milking.

In calving season, it was our job to feed the calves. We would collect milk from the vat and get the herd together. We even had jobs to do when they were butchered, which was just part of everyday life.

It's something that I regret my children haven't been able to experience. I wouldn't change my upbringing for the world.

The other thing I realise is that for my uncle and aunty, taking me on when Nan and Pop needed a break was a big commitment. Aunty Bronwyn and Uncle George had four children already and, although I wasn't a full-on whāngai for them, I would still have been a lot of work and an extra mouth to feed. I'm very grateful to them and I'm still very close to those cousins.

There were times I felt like I was a hindrance to them. I knew my parents were in Auckland and I hoped they were contributing to my running expenses. Aunty bought my clothes. Nan would help. I was aware of that responsibility even at a young age. I shouldn't have worried about it, but I did. I was so happy with everything I was getting.

He tina ki runga, he tāmore ki raro

———————————

Contentment above, firmly rooted below

CHAPTER TWO

GROWING UP FAST

PAWARENGA is a predominantly Catholic area and my first schooling was at Hata Maria (Saint Mary) convent school, where I was taught by nuns. People now think about nuns as something from the olden days, but they were a very real presence in my childhood. I went to the local intermediate school after that and then on to Hato Petera in Auckland for high school, where I became a boarder. I was a full-timer, only going back to Pawarenga at the end of term for the school holidays. We had weekends off, but Sunday was also for church and catching up on schoolwork.

Hato Petera was an old school that had helped Catholic Māori boys get a good education since 1928, when it opened. By the time I got there, it was helping Catholic Māori girls as well. It was open to everyone, but the emphasis on Māori culture alongside the Catholic religion was a big part of its mission. Many Catholic children from up north were sent there for their secondary education. (Sadly, it closed in 2010.)

Hato Petera was yet another new world for me and I loved it. My family supported me financially to go there and at the end of my first year I won the Lang Davis Memorial Scholarship. It was set up to honour a former principal and I had the honour of being the first person to get it. I don't know what I did to earn it, and only found out about it at prize-giving. But it paid for everything, and was a big help to the whānau. I was proud that I was able to show that they had been right to put their faith in me.

Of course, I missed Nan and Pop and my Proctor family, but at Hato Petera we had dorm parents to keep an eye out for us. They act like your mother and father while you are at school. Mine were two wonderful people: Hori and Steph Pirini. They were originally from Pawarenga too, and I could talk to them about anything. It really helped having people who knew my background so well. Later, I had Wero and Damian Campbell.

Dorm parents had to be special people to look after a whole bunch of teenage boys and girls who were a long way from home. They helped us with cooking and cleaning and budgeting and any other problems we had. One kid kept getting into fights, another one was being bullied and many of us came from broken families. There was a whole range of teenage troubles and they took them all in their stride.

One of the first things our dorm parents did when we came down to boarding school – and one of the best things – was put all the new students in a van and take us around town to show us the city. I'd already seen some of it on my visits to Mum, but this was a full-on tour of all the important sights.

And we got to look at prostitutes as well, and got told what they do, and that was neat. A lot of us were surprised that so many of them were fairly elderly women. We thought that was very interesting.

I think Hato Petera used to be quite a strict boarding school, like you see on TV and movies. But when girls started attending the school, things eased up a bit and the discipline wasn't as military as it had been. As long as we asked our dorm parents, we could leave the grounds and go to the shop any time we wanted.

And the 'dorms' weren't old style ones in big buildings with rows of beds, but five kāinga around the school. A lot of people driving past them wouldn't even have realised they had anything to do with the school.

We had prayers in the chapel every night at seven and after that you went back to the dorm to finish your homework before bed.

In my later years, when I became a senior, I got my own room and that was one of the best times of my life. Our bedrooms had their own en suite bathrooms. That meant showers with hot water. For me, it was almost too good to be true. I was always afraid the hot water would run out, so I used to have a shower in the morning and another at night. That's a habit I have to this day.

In many people's eyes, it probably wasn't very flash at all, but to us kids from the country it was beautiful. In fact, when the roll started to fall – there were only thirty-five pupils left when the school closed in 2018 – the rooms were good enough to be rented out to students from the nearby Auckland University of Technology.

IT'S PROBABLY AS WELL that I had been exposed to tangi up north, because attending them was part of our mahi as students. The boys were often expected to turn up at a funeral and do a haka, especially if it was a big important one.

I didn't mind, because it got me out of the classroom, I got to see more of the big smoke – which was still a novelty to me – and

I got to learn a bit about what kinds of jobs there were out in the world.

I did a lot of kapa haka. I had done a fair bit up north at both primary and intermediate school, so it was one of my favourite things anyway, but I loved being able to do so much of it. Our groups were invited to perform at lots of corporate events and business functions. The school had a good relationship with Stephen Tindall and The Warehouse, so every time a new Warehouse opened we'd go along and do the blessing ceremony.

Part of it was like blessing a house when it is new. It's also something you do after a funeral. You walk around the whole place, touching everything as you go. Some of these Warehouses were massive, and having to walk up and down all the aisles doing the blessing took ages. But it was great because they always gave a good donation to the school.

This was next-level kapa haka compared to what I'd done at Pawarenga. The school competed in Polyfest and took it seriously, so our practices were hard out. I loved it. I loved music anyway, so it fitted with that interest. And for energetic teenagers, it's a good way to keep them occupied and out of trouble when they don't have schoolwork to do.

But just sometimes in the middle of kapa haka I would think: *Why the heck am I doing this? How is this going to help me in my chosen field of work, whatever that ends up being?* Because I certainly had no idea then what I wanted to do with my life.

But I kept it up and thank goodness I did, because I learnt a lot that has helped me in my chosen field. I especially learnt about focus, hard work and cooperation. Later, I would find that running a business is like doing a company kapa haka – you have to discipline yourselves, work as a team and concentrate on the bigger picture rather than the immediate outcome. Those are the principles and foundations of kapa haka, which is beautiful.

I loved kapa haka most, but I also had to play regular sports. I wasn't very good at league or rugby but I played them anyway. And every morning there was someone banging on the doors and yelling at us to get up and go for a run. Whatever else I got at school, I got fit.

And I was competitive enough to keep going. I always wanted to win, even if I didn't have a chance.

I was also in demand to play the guitar at various events. Without TV and other entertainment options in Pawarenga, making music had been part of our life. Pop was an avid guitarist who often sat and picked away. When it was time for me to go to bed, he brought the guitar out, sat on a little stool and played for me until he thought I was asleep.

'Don't stop, Pop,' I'd say. 'Keep playing.'

And he would. I think the sound of the guitar stays with you. Kaiora and I did that with Nikora, our eldest. He loves the guitar too. I missed that with the other kids but I've started it again with the new baby.

There was also a lot of wonderful singing in my early life. The old kuia who sang at church on Sunday made the most beautiful sound. Being able to listen to them was a great joy. And they were complete naturals. When we do kapa haka, we are organised: sopranos here, tenors there. But these old women seemed to know their harmonies by instinct and when they lifted up their voices they turned that tiny wooden chapel on the hill into the most beautiful cathedral.

That's the result you yearn for when you're doing kapa haka – all those notes coming together to make one magnificent sound.

A lot of those ladies are dead now, but the imprint they left in our hearts is something special. We didn't really understand the words but we loved the tunes and harmonies. When I went to Hato Petera, we sang all the songs they had sung – and as I learnt a bit more te reo Māori and had religious studies, I also learnt about what those songs really meant. If you understand what you are singing about, it changes it. Those old kuia certainly did.

AS FOR SOCIAL LIFE and friends – no one will get you into as much trouble as your friends will. I was always the good boy, but some of my friends weren't quite so good, which is how I got to have my first joint. The others would often be stoned at school – boys and girls.

'Don't you want some?' I got asked one day.

'No, I might get in trouble. I'll lose my scholarship. My nan will be so angry.'

'No one will ever find out.'

'Are you sure?' Because I was really dying to try it.

So we went down the back of the school and they gave me some weed. It was so neat. I couldn't inhale or do the smoking bit, but I figured it all out later. Suck it in, hold it, let the smoke out.

'I don't feel anything,' I said after about thirty seconds.

'Have some more then.'

I had some more.

'I still don't feel anything.'

They gave me some more. This was around 6.30 pm and it was my job to play the guitar for evening prayers at 7 pm. And not just a couple of tunes, but the pre-prayers, kapa haka and hymns. By the time we got to the chapel, I was stoned off my face. I wasn't the only one who was stoned, but I was the only one who was going to have to play the guitar.

'Francis, we're going to have this hymn,' said Mr Leef.

I looked at my friends and they were all so happy. They were loving this. I started to play a different hymn from the one I'd been told to play.

'What the hell!' exploded Mr Leef. 'That's not what I told you to play. Are you stoned?'

How did he know?

'I'm so sorry, sir,' I said, 'I'll never do it again.'

I got such a fright, but then I realised he was joking, because there was no way good little Francis would be stoned at prayers. I thought he was angry at me for being stoned, but he was angry because I was playing the wrong hymn. And my friends were all calling out, offering to play it because they were worried I'd slip up and give them away. They were swearing at me under their breath to just shut the F-word up.

I got there in the end, but it took a lot longer than usual. (And for anyone who's worried, you'll find out later that I became a Mormon, so not only do I have a life free of weed, it's also free of alcohol, nicotine and caffeine. And I play the right song on the guitar every time.)

I was never going to be top of the class. I liked social studies – learning about different parts of the world and the different ways people do things – and I loved geography. I didn't really like English, but when it came time to sit School Certificate the only subjects I passed were English and Māori.

Well, a definite blessing I got out of school was my oldest son, Haimona, who was born in early 2001. Hato Petera had boys' dorms and girls' dorms, but one of the things about them being in houses was that it was pretty easy to get from one house to another and to meet up with the girls.

Pa Tate, the school chaplain, was a wonderful priest – also from up north. When he heard I got a girl pregnant, he went to the chapel, lit a candle, sent someone to get me and sat there waiting.

I was in my dorm when one of the boys came to my room: 'You have to go and see Pa Tate.'

'Oh good,' I thought, because I did so well playing for things that every time there was a special mass or function he would want to see me to talk about what hymns would be played and so that I could organise the altar boys and girls. I got over to the chapel as it was getting dark. When I arrived, he was sitting up at the altar with his back to the door. I walked in and genuflected.

'Kia ora, Pa.'

'Haere mai,' he said. 'Come and sit here.'

So I walked up and sat down next to him.

'Look, you know why we're here,' he said.

'No, Pa.'

Then he spoke about the pregnancy, talking in te reo the whole time.

'With this,' he said, 'comes responsibilities. You have to think about the pēpi coming.' And he described just some of the things that I would have to do if I was going to be responsible for a new life.

I thought he was going to blast me, but it wasn't a growling; it was advice. He wasn't going to waste time focusing on all the bad things I'd been doing. He was concerned about making

I was always the good boy, but some of my friends weren't quite so good, which is how I got to have my first joint. The others would often be stoned at school – boys and girls.

sure everything was going to be okay. My appreciation for him changed. He said he was disappointed because he had seen a bright future for me.

After that, all he wanted me to do was repent and make my confession. I confessed about the sneaking around, and I chucked a few more things in, then he made me do a decade of the rosary and that was that. Official part over.

And the strangest thing was, even though it was really uncomfortable, when I came away I felt like he was looking after me like a dad father, not like a priest father.

Haimona was baptised in the chapel at Hato Petera. I had already left school and I worked as a postie for a while, and was glad I was able to provide food and clothing for my family and pay the rent. I had to grow up pretty quickly at the age of seventeen.

Not surprisingly, my relationship with Haimona's mum didn't last long and we soon broke up. We were too young to know much about anything and it was never likely to work out. But I'm grateful for my son Haimona.

KAIORA'S STORY

Kaiora: In some ways, I had a similar upbringing to my husband, Francis. Like the Tipene family, we were poor but rich in tikanga. But unlike Francis, I was one of a big family of twelve brothers and sisters, and my parents stayed together, although my father died young, at the age of just fifty-one.

My dad never listened when it came to health. He was very stubborn. He had a list of foods he was supposed to eat, but he ignored it. If he wanted to eat wild pork, he would. Mutton bird, he would. He ate all the foods you're not supposed to eat. But it was traditional kai, so for him he was being true to himself.

I was ten when he died. Mum is still alive. She is a matriarch and she raised us on her own for many years and she's done a marvellous job for all of us.

My father had become a well-known and respected kaumātua in the north and made claims to belonging to or being connected to every iwi up there. He was very vocal. He had strong connections with Hone Harawira, Sir Graham Latimer and many of the people of the north.

If there was a tangi or anything like that, he would be available to act as the kaumātua.

Many people in the area knew him. It was out of the ordinary if he didn't show up at a tangi. We went to nearly every funeral that took place.

After school, all you want to do is play with your friends but we often found ourselves at the marae, sitting down and being quiet. We couldn't do anything till our dad did a mihi, then we had to sing a song, and that's when we were allowed to go and play bullrush. But that was where I did all my early learning about tangi, without realising how important they would become in my life.

I got a lot of knowledge from him – knowing when to speak, knowing my place and where I should be on a marae, or even in a space where you sense tikanga is being practised.

We just observed and absorbed, although we got a whack if we tried to sneak away. The younger kids were allowed to go out and play but the older siblings had to help in the kitchen.

If we didn't want to learn or be part of the marae processes, then we had to make ourselves useful outside. If we were being part of what was going on, we had to stay and sing a waiata for Aunty So and So, or tautoko Uncle So and So.

My father taught us that you weren't allowed to stand on a marae unless you could whakapapa to it. He had great knowledge in whakapapa and he tried to pass it on to us. My elder siblings learnt more from him than I did, but even now when I meet people I often recognise the names and know who they are from what he taught me.

He would drill us with names of our connections up north. He taught us karanga and about tikanga and kawa. That meant when I met Francis we connected straight away on that level because we both knew a lot about it.

My brothers tried to fill our father's shoes but it was very difficult. The eldest was twenty-three when Dad died, the next twenty-one, and so on, every two years all the way down to me.

Our dad was our pou. He gave us advice and told us what needed to happen every day, so when he died we didn't know what to do. We didn't continue those practices. If someone passed away, we'd go to a tangi once a month, not twice a week. People still remembered who we were but we didn't remember them, and we lost some connections with our people.

It's a mixed blessing being the offspring of a kaumātua. You get a lot of respect but with that comes a lot of obligation. Even now, when I meet people, it's amazing how they remember my dad and share the experiences they had with him.

*

I THINK WHEN FRANCIS was growing up, he was probably a bit better off than my family in terms of necessities. We had no power either, but with twelve of us things had to be spread a lot more thinly. I had a lot of hand-me-downs as a child.

The first eight of my siblings were brought up in Puapua, two hours south-west of Kaitaia. As well as having no electricity, we had no running water. If you wanted a shower, you washed in the creek. If you wanted a warm bath, you had to collect your own water and heat it. Mum would sometimes dig holes in the ground to keep food cold.

That was the upbringing the eldest eight had. Then we moved to Kaitaia and the youngest four – including me – got to enjoy the benefits of electricity and other basics.

Puapua became our holiday home, but by the time we left there I had learnt about the simple life and how to be grateful for what we had.

It wasn't always fun, but it was good for me because it means I am very good with money. I don't waste a penny and I don't want things we don't need. I'm frugal and I save. Francis loves that. He thinks if I were any different and we both treated money the way he does, we'd have gone under by now. And I'm absolutely sure he is right.

Sometimes I get a little sad about how little we had and how I used to scab food from kids at school. I thought a tub of yoghurt or a little packet of chips was the most amazing thing ever. We never had anything like that.

Sometimes, other kids laughed at me because I didn't have those sorts of treats in my lunch. Or if they found out we didn't have a TV at home. And then I just felt really small.

Francis tries to turn those things into positives. 'Mum, it's made you who you are today,' he says. (He calls me Mum, I think because we have all these other males in the house who call me Mum, so it's just easier.)

He thinks it would be good for our kids to have to go without a yoghurt in their school lunch, especially when he sees the lunchboxes come back with them only half eaten. Not that he would ever deny the kids.

I HAVE SOMETHING ELSE in common with Francis – Pawarenga. My family has some land there. Dad bought the whenua and made himself known there.

But getting together with Francis when the time came was a big no-no for my family because they didn't want me to have anything to do with someone from Pawarenga.

The problem was that my brother had built a whare at the top of the hill and one of the locals burnt it down. Because of that, my brothers had a lot of hate on nearly everybody there.

It had happened because we got in the way of a lot of the drug trade that was going on. If you went there, you would take one look and say: 'This place is a gold mine for drugs.' And it was.

My brother didn't want any of that happening on his land so he set fire to a lot of patches and destroyed them. And his home got burnt down in retaliation.

Francis and I were courting at the time that happened, and I kept thinking: *How am I going to tell my whānau I want to be with someone from this place?* Even though he was obviously not someone who would have had anything to do with that kind of stuff.

But my brothers still did the big standover anyway.

They cornered Francis once at our place in Kaitaia. They weren't intending to. He was just there to meet everybody and ask for my hand in marriage. I introduced him: 'Hi, everybody, this is my darling. He's Francis Tipene –'

My brother saw red and shot out of his seat when he heard Francis's name.

'You're Francis Tipene? From Pawarenga? You want to bring your Pawarenga ways into our family? … If you want to bring your Pawarenga ways here … Don't you come along with your Pawarenga ways because we will …'

I was so embarrassed and I felt really stink because he had just been trying to do the right thing. This was my sweetheart. They had it all wrong. I explained who exactly his family were, and it wasn't quite so bad when my whānau understood which whānau he belonged to.

They are apologetic about it to this day.

But that's the Māori way: get things out in the open and deal with them as soon as possible.

And once it was sorted – and they knew I was pregnant – they wanted us to get married tomorrow, no mucking around.

He hono tangata e kore e motu,
kā pā, he taura waka e motu

———————————

A human bond is unbreakable,
unlike the severable canoe rope

CHAPTER THREE

FRANCIS AND KAIORA

I ENROLLED IN Te Wānanga Takiura o Ngā Kura Kaupapa Māori o Aotearoa in Auckland. It was a training college for people who wanted to become teachers and work in kura kaupapa. I was twenty when I began a year of learning to get my language skills up. I had learnt a lot of te reo Māori at school but by now there was a lot about the language I needed to be updated on. Technology had grown and there were lots of new words to learn.

I did that for a year. And a beautiful young woman called Kaiora Murray was also a student there and in some of my classes. I thought she was out of my league (and she was).

Not only that, she was going out with the owner's son. This guy was a bit of a know-it-all and somewhat intimidating. While I was attending Hato Petera, there was an annual speech competition called Ngā Manu Kōrero – for the very best of the best Māori speech makers – and he always won it. I saw them dating while attending Te Wānanga Takiura and I just always hoped she noticed me. I thought maybe if I got up at the whānau hui gatherings that were held weekly at Takiura and gave the best speech, I would catch her eye.

And I didn't find out till later but she had noticed me, even though she knew nothing about me. She told me she liked the way I took pride in my appearance and that I could sing. And she especially liked the fact that I was fluent in te reo Māori and understood and loved our traditions. I was grateful to my upbringing for that. And she thought I had a lot of confidence – even though I didn't think I did.

I tried a few times to get up at whānau hui gatherings, but that guy was in a different league from me and I knew I would never get there. That was okay, I just carried on with life – studying and partying.

As the months went on, I realised she and that guy weren't hanging out any more and I heard they were no longer a couple.

I had grown up a lot in the meantime. My son was a toddler now, and looking after a baby definitely makes you grow up fast. Unless you're not a responsible person at heart – then it's a disaster.

I think Kaiora saw me more as a man than a boy. In fact, she said I looked like I was thirty-five – 'a kaumātua in a young man's body' is how she described it. And I was only twenty. Anyway, that worked in my favour.

One night there was a party where we had planned to meet up. There was a misunderstanding when Kaiora couldn't find me at the party. In the end, she left without telling anyone and I got very frustrated when I went looking for her and couldn't find her.

The next day I tried to call her. I think there were eighteen missed calls before she finally noticed and called me back. And then I missed her call.

Next day I rang to find out what happened and she said she thought I had been with another girl. And we started talking properly like grown-ups to each other. We talked for two hours about relationships in general, and we were sharing some serious things.

'Come round, and if you're really interested we can talk about it properly,' she said. I went round to her place and stayed and stayed. Apparently, she thought I smelt really good and that was when she fell in love with me. We've been together ever since.

'Will your mum be wondering where you are?' she joked one day, after about two straight weeks together. It was her way of saying I could go home to my mum's house if I wanted to. But I didn't. And luckily, she didn't get sick of me. And still hasn't.

I was the happiest guy after that. I thought I hit the jackpot. We became an item and moved in together. It was a very different relationship from the one I had come out of, because I was older and knew the mistakes I had made before.

With a first relationship, especially if you're a teenager, you're not really sure of life or anything else and that's where you do a lot of learning. This time, because I thought Kaiora was wonderful and I knew I wanted to be with her forever, we talked about what we wanted out of the relationship.

The first three months is playing around getting to know each other. After that, and realising we loved each other, we had to figure out what to do next. What were our goals?

One of the first was to get married at some point, because our son Nikora was on the way. But whether he had been coming or not, I wanted to marry her to seal the deal. I wasn't in any hurry, though.

We knew we both wanted to work, not just to provide the basics but to have our own home. That was one of our goals right from the start – and we're still working on that one.

There was one small complication, which was that Kaiora belonged to the Mormon faith, which was not in line with Catholicism. We didn't think about that too much when we were courting. I didn't know anything about Mormons or what they believed. And Kaiora hadn't exactly been leading a strict Mormon lifestyle at that point. She was brought up in the church but became less active – that's how we met. It's ironic that Mormons don't drink, because if it hadn't been for alcohol at one party, I probably would never have worked up the courage to talk to someone so beautiful.

She had mentioned her faith, but I wasn't really interested and didn't pay much attention. I was more interested in getting her to come to my church with me and see how Catholics did things.

Then one night, she said, 'Honey, can I have a prayer?'

'Okay,' I said, even though I was used to praying in church or at big gatherings, not just at home with someone else.

And when she started her prayer, it was like listening to another person. It was the most beautiful thing I'd ever heard. We had been living this regular student lifestyle of a bit of work plus parties and drinking and dope, then all of a sudden Kaiora was talking a language that sounded like it came from Heaven. You could tell she was talking directly to God and it was all about thanking thee for thy many blessings and other such old-fashioned language.

I thought: *Where did this come from?*

Together, we either spoke regular English or te reo Māori.

Now there was this third language. I began to tear up, and by the end of her prayer I was weeping.

And that led me to let down my defences and want to know more about a church that could create something so beautiful.

All my life, I had seen the guys in suits riding bikes around in pairs and wondered what they were about. I thought they were salespeople. She explained to me about the missionaries and how every young Mormon male has to devote two years to missionary work, often in another country.

'Would you like to hear what they have to say?' said Kaiora.

'Sure.'

She never pressured me, but the invitation was there. So we invited them to our home in Te Atatu. They talked me through the simple lessons about the church, ending with baptism. I was blown away. I was converted. I wanted to become a Mormon then and there.

But they wouldn't let me rush into it. They said I should pray and ask for guidance, not just rely on what they said. So I did and felt overcome by a beautiful feeling I couldn't really explain. Kaiora also encouraged me to pray and find out for myself, because she wanted me to do it for me, not for her or anyone else. She said lately she would have married me even if I hadn't converted.

But the thing that really convinced me that this was what I wanted was one particular lesson. I learnt that if I married Kaiora as a Mormon, we would be together for eternity – not just in this life but forever. And that made me so happy, because I loved her so much.

Before I made the decision to convert, I met Kaiora's mother and that was when stuff got serious.

Obviously, we couldn't put off telling her about the baby forever – especially if Kaiora ever wanted to see her mother. Kaiora already knew how this was going to work, but she didn't tell me, which was probably just as well or I might not have been so happy to go along with it.

I had finished my one-year course at Te Wānanga, but Kaiora's three-year degree there would be interrupted. We decided the baby was more important and this was just a pause. One day, she would come back and finish her training.

One day, she still might.

We settled on a night to break the news to her mother when she was visiting Auckland. The plan was to take her out for dinner first and give her the news, then go to a movie to take everyone's minds off things. She thought she was getting dinner and a movie, but actually she was getting dinner and a movie and a baby.

Dinner was in a food hall because we were students: chicken and fried rice was the best we could do.

We ordered our food, and then it was time to talk.

'Mum, we've got something to tell you,' said Kaiora. Then she looked at me and said, 'You tell her.'

I took a deep breath. 'Kaiora is pregnant.'

'Okay,' said her mother.

That's all she said for a long time. She would be great at poker.

'So, what now?' she said at last.

'We are going to have a baby.'

'So, what now?'

'Well, we're going to the movies after this.'

'Okay. And then what?'

I didn't understand what she was getting at for ages. What she meant was: when are you going to put a ring on my daughter's hand? She definitely wanted it to be before the baby was born.

Eventually she had to spell it out for me and said: 'When are you going to marry my daughter?'

That took me by surprise, because marriage any time soon wasn't in my thinking, although I definitely wanted it to happen one day.

'As soon as possible,' I said, but I didn't mean *soon* soon. I just meant soonish. I said it because it was all I could think of.

And there were some more 'And then whats?' until I realised that as far as my new mother-in-law was concerned, she meant baptism. Her daughter was going to marry a Mormon, not a Catholic.

We got to the movie in the end, but I can't remember what it was or anything that happened in it, and I'm sure no one else would be able to either. All our minds were racing, going through all the possible scenarios and what would have to be organised now it wasn't just about a baby but about a wedding and a baptism as well.

I thought: *What have I just done?*

Marriage was so common in Nan and Pop's generation, but not as common in the generation after them.

Nan's reaction was definitely on my mind. I knew she was going to be angry, and at first I thought I would just tell her about the wedding and leave out the bit about converting to Mormonism. But I told her on the phone one day and it went just as well as I thought it would.

'Don't do it,' she yelled when I told her I was going to be baptised as a Mormon. 'I'll disown you. If you do it, you'll never talk to me again.'

I was sad. This was supposed to be a joyous occasion and Nan was spoiling it for me. But then I thought about what things were like back in her day, when people were even more judgmental and there were stigmas about bastard children and so on.

And then I got annoyed, because it was 2005 and I was having to put up with this in the twenty-first century between two mothers who came from a completely different generation to me, and who had very strict ideas that weren't my ideas.

BEFORE WE MARRIED, we moved back up north, because Kaiora wanted to be close to her mother when the baby came. Having had twelve children, she would know just about all there was to know about having a baby.

Even though she has two younger brothers, Kaiora is the youngest girl in her family, so she is still the baby in everyone's eyes – and they all want to protect her. This was a case of her mum's baby having a baby.

We both found jobs in Kaitaia. She was working at the kōhanga reo and I was doing training for the local iwi. When we moved there, my pregnant fiancée and I stayed with her mother – in separate bedrooms, in single beds. That was just the way it was as far as a devout Mormon mum was concerned. Maybe she was worried that if we slept together, Kaiora would have twins.

The night before the wedding was one of the most embarrassing of my life. Kaiora had her hen night at her sister's place and was staying there. And I had a stag night with my mother-in-law.

She took me out to buy a double bed. We went to a local second-hand shop, and it was just so awkward. I realise it was

When each of our children
was born, she snuck up
to their cribs with a little
bit of holy water and
made the sign of the cross
on their heads with it.
It makes her happy.

practical, but it was a little bit gross. And the bed we ended up getting was a blow-up one. Well, at least Kaiora and I were finally allowed to sleep next to each other, even if it was on an inflatable mattress.

The wedding took place at the registry office in the courthouse in Kaitaia. It was pretty simple, with just whānau and close friends attending. We sang 'Whakaaria Mai' and a lovely justice of the peace married us.

'Do you have any rings to exchange?' he said, when the time came.

'No,' we both replied and just held each other's hands. There were no rings because we couldn't afford them. We had only just moved towns and changed jobs and we hadn't even had our first pay. Then a good friend of ours stood up and took a ring off her finger.

'Give this to your wife,' she said to me. I was so touched.

We were happy. It probably wasn't what my nan wanted, and that did matter to me. I understood she would have liked to have a big affair and make it a very special occasion, but I just wanted to do the process and hurry up and be able to say: 'This is my wife.'

Afterwards we went to a popular Chinese takeaway and restaurant, the Sea Dragon, and had a little reception with some good kōrero. There was no honeymoon; we just carried on with our daily lives and went back to work.

I was baptised as a member of the Mormon faith, in a full immersion ceremony at the Latter-day Saints Chapel in Kaitaia. Kaiora and a lot of other people were there to support me – and make sure I went right under.

We've also been to the Temple near Hamilton, which is a goal for all Mormons, and been sealed to be together for all eternity.

I love the principles the church gives us to live by. It's not always easy to follow the rules around coffee, alcohol, smoking and so on. But if it was easy, we wouldn't be human.

THE BARRIERS between our families and their religions didn't stay up for long. Once Nikora was born, both sides quickly came together. I had put the difference to the back of my mind and waited for everyone to come around. I knew my nan would come back one day and it would all be okay. She did and it has. She came to the wedding (but not my baptism) and has even been to a few of our Mormon activity nights, which are great occasions where everyone has fun without alcohol. We play games and have performances. It's showed Nan that Mormons are people, not some weird cult.

Nan had once been upset that I was converting from Catholicism and marrying a Morman, but it's all settled down now. Except for one little thing. When each of our children was born, she snuck up to their cribs with a little bit of holy water and made the sign of the cross on their heads with it. It makes her happy, so my wife and I leave her to it. That might cause problems in some families, but it's got to make her feel better. She needs to do it and we understand the history and reasons.

Babies are amazing for the way they have of bringing people together, and the circumstances of how Nikora came into this world made everyone very aware he was a special child. Kaiora will tell you about it.

MEETING NIKORA

Kaiora: When you have your first baby, you have no expectations. You've never done it before so you don't know if what is happening is the right thing or not. You assume everything is okay because all the people around you are professionals with plenty of experience.

The midwife I had for most of my first pregnancy is no longer practising. I wasn't the only person who had a very bad experience with her. And I didn't know ninety-six hours of contractions wasn't normal.

I had been okay all through my pregnancy. And the labour seemed to start okay, but after forty-eight hours of strong contractions twenty minutes apart with nothing happening, I would have thought she might have got concerned.

Instead, she told me she had to go to a conference and a new midwife came in for the third 24-hour period. This midwife decided I needed to go to Whangarei Hospital because Kaitaia didn't have the resources to look after me and my baby.

Francis, Mum and I headed off on a nightmare of a drive. It normally takes a couple of hours but took a lot longer because I needed to stop all the time. My sister Ngawaiata, who also lived in Kaitaia, arranged to meet us in Whangarei.

Now I was being dealt with by yet another bunch of people who hadn't been there through the whole process, so I had to start all over again. I expected I'd be taken straight into the theatre but the specialist had a whole lot of questions. She wasn't happy that we had just turned up and she didn't know what was going on.

Also, she was hapū as.

'You're five months pregnant and you think you're going to work on my daughter like that?' said my mum. 'No way. Is there anyone else who can work on her?' She wasn't going to take anything for granted.

The staff wanted me to keep waiting, even after all that time, in the hope that I might have a natural birth. But it wasn't going to happen.

We finally made it to the emergency room, and my son was delivered by Caesarean after ninety-six hours.

But I didn't hear him cry. When a baby is born, you want to hear that little tangi, but there was no tangi at all. The only thing I could hear was whispering with the midwife.

They wheeled my boy around so I could see him and said: 'Congratulations, here's your son. Now we're just going to pop off for a second.' And they wheeled him away again.

I was lying there exhausted and I was very upset.

'Where's my son going?' I said.

Francis had left for a moment then come back again and he was crying. I didn't like him crying. He wasn't the one whose tangi I wanted to hear.

'I need you to remain calm,' the doctor said.

That was it.

'Don't tell me to remain calm!' And suddenly I was crying too. I didn't like not knowing what was happening, and I was scared.

'We may need to take your son to Starship Hospital in Auckland,' said the doctor. 'He is not breathing properly and we're doing the best we can to help him breathe. We need to take you to the recovery room, then we will take you up to baby and if needs be at some point you will both be shipped to Starship.'

It was awful. I couldn't stop crying.

Ngawaiata was with me when we went into the recovery room, but Francis went off to see if he could find out more about what was happening to baby. He was trying to get through all these doors and emergency exits that had security locks and then there was a power cut so they wouldn't open or close at all.

I noticed I was feeling faint and starting to shut down a little bit. Then the doctors noticed a lot of blood gushing out. I had been stitched up after the birth but I was losing blood and they didn't know where it was coming from.

More doctors came into the room. They asked my sister to leave.

'We need time to assess your sister,' said one. 'She may need to go back to theatre.'

My sister wasn't into that. She got dramatic on them.

'Her husband's not here,' she said, 'and I'm not going anywhere, and you need to fix what's happening.'

'It's important that we can do our work,' explained a doctor. 'And we're not going to do an emergency procedure in front of you.'

And then she started crying, so I had to be the calm one.

'No, no, don't cry,' I said. 'Please leave. I'm coming back.'

So she went out.

'You'd better make sure she comes back,' I heard her say to the doctors as she went out. I didn't like hearing that. I could feel the doctors stabbing away at me trying to put in an IV. They couldn't do it, but I could see bags of blood being brought in.

'Am I dying?' I asked a doctor.

'There is some complication, but I can't have you die on my watch,' she said.

Francis had found his way back and kissed me as I was being wheeled into theatre. We all did a lot of praying together in those hours. The experience tested our faith a lot and we poured our hearts and souls out to our heavenly father asking him to help us.

Francis kissed me on my head and whispered, 'You come back to me.'

The last straw for him was that just before I went into theatre, he had to sign an indemnity form in case anything went wrong when they were operating and I died. He signed and said: 'Save her life.'

And I could hear the rest of my family calling from the other side of the screen: 'Baby, baby, you come back to Mummy, you hear.' And I started to tear up. *Why was my family talking to me like this?* I didn't like it.

Within moments, I blacked out. When I came around again, I was out of theatre and in the intensive care unit.

'Oh my goodness,' said a nurse, laughing away, 'you were a case and a half for me last night.'

'Where's my family?' I asked.

'They're on their way. I've told them you're here.'

'Good. Can you tell them I'm so hungry, I need McDonald's.'

'No, no, no – you're not allowed to eat for at least another four hours.'

'What? Can I have anything?'

'There's water. You need to sip on that.'

It was like torture. They explained I had lost eleven litres of blood and they had to pump sixteen litres into me. And they had nearly given me a hysterectomy.

'You're lucky – this shouldn't restrict the number of children you have.'

I was so grateful to know I would be able to have another baby. Not that I was thinking much about that at the time. Just looking at a pregnant woman was painful. My sister was due four weeks after me and every time I saw her I groaned.

'I've performed nine C-sections on one mother, so you should know it's possible to have as many children as you want,' the doctor said.

'I'm not having nine!'

It turned out that, because the labour had gone on so long, my body had been put under such strain that my uterus had torn, and that was where the blood had been coming from.

I was still able to get pregnant and have my babies, and have had four more, but they all have to be Caesareans performed two weeks before the due date. I can't be allowed to go into labour in case the old tear gets ripped open again.

It wasn't until I was released from intensive care forty-eight hours after the delivery that I got to hold my son. No one else had been allowed to. The family wanted me to hold him first. I was grateful for that, but mainly I was just grateful to have him at all.

I found out he hadn't been breathing for a long time and because the labour had been allowed to go on for so long, he had started to choke on meconium. The doctors were surprised at how well he did. They checked him every six weeks for the first part of his life.

There'd been a high risk of brain damage, but we were lucky and he came through it all okay. There were no signs of deafness, blindness or brain damage. He was responding perfectly. They couldn't believe this baby who hadn't been breathing for nearly an hour had recovered so well.

Many years later, Francis had to deal with the case of a girl who had died in pregnancy from much the same thing that we had lived through. It was almost exactly what had happened to me, but this girl hadn't survived and he had to console the young father. I know he found that very hard.

Mā Puhimoanaariki koe hei mau

———————————

May you be guided by the great Puhimoanaariki

CHAPTER FOUR

A FUTURE IN FUNERALS

IN KAITAIA with our new baby, I was still teaching tikanga, waiata and kapa haka in the schools and Kaiora was working as a kaiako at a kōhanga reo. I loved it. Part of the work involved attending tangi and helping with the tangihanga ceremonies. Whenever someone who was Māori died, we as a Māori organisation went along to support each other. After I'd done this a hundred or so times, my interest had grown to the point where I decided it was what I wanted to do with my life.

'Baby, I really want to start my own business,' I told Kaiora.

'Okay, honey. Sweet as,' she said.

'I'm going to start my own funeral home.'

'Cool.'

I could tell she was stunned, but I didn't let on. I knew she was hoping it was just talk and by the end of the week I would have decided there was something else I wanted to do. But I went ahead on my own and did some research.

I rang around companies to see if they'd be open to employing me and letting them know what I could bring to them in terms of my knowledge of tikanga. Obviously, I couldn't just start my own firm with no experience, though I knew I wanted to be my own boss one day. First, I had to learn about being a funeral director – and the only way to do that is on the job. One of the companies I contacted said they would give me an interview, and by the end of the week I had an offer.

'Honey, I've found a job with a funeral director in Auckland. Martin Williams Funeral Directors in Papatoetoe will let me work for them.'

Now Kaiora had to take it seriously.

'What about me and baby and a place to stay?' she asked.

'I've also found us a place to stay and a job for you at the local kura.'

'Whoa – that is serious,' she said.

We had to move for me to follow my dream. Kaitaia is a small town and the established funeral director there had the business to himself. Naturally he wasn't going to offer me a job and train me up to be his opposition one day.

So we packed up Nikora and moved back to Auckland.

In my early days with Martin Williams in Papatoetoe I was mainly doing police work. That meant working on behalf of the coroner and police to pick up bodies in cases of unexpected sudden deaths – car crash, suicide, homicide. Anything that a doctor couldn't just write out a death certificate for.

That is the rough end of the business, and after three months I wasn't sure I wanted to do it. It really wasn't what I had signed up for. I was more into the ceremony of funerals, embalming the dead and dealing with the living. And I did get to do a little bit of that, but even then, it was mainly reconstructive work where a body had been badly damaged.

I thought sometimes, *Am I really seeing this?*, as I looked at what was left of a person lying in front of me.

Once, when someone had been hit by a train on the tracks near Otahuhu, I was walking along the line picking up body parts and not feeling good about it. It wasn't the dream I had had, but at the same time, I knew someone had to do this job for this poor person, and that thought kept me going. I was doing just a little bit to help restore that person's dignity and mana. I worked that out for myself and that thought kept me going in the early days. If I hadn't been able to see that, I'd have probably given it all away.

So I'm glad I got given that awful job to do right at the start. In the funeral industry, if you can do that work, you can do anything because you've already seen it all.

Kaiora was at home with our young baby and finances were a struggle – a junior funeral director doesn't get paid very much. We were renting a house in Manurewa, and not in a good part. On one side was an alleyway where all sorts of people could slink around out of sight. We got broken into three times while we were living there. Once, burglars broke a window when Kaiora and Nikora were at home. We made it work because it was all we could afford.

Eventually, I left Martin Williams because I wanted to get more involved in Māori funerals and there was an opportunity with Lagoon View Funeral Services in Panmure.

Lagoon View predominantly did Māori funerals. That's when I really began to feel comfortable in my role as a funeral director. I learnt more skills – such as removals (when the deceased is

I'm glad I got given that awful job to do right at the start. In the funeral industry, if you can do that work, you can do anything because you've already seen it all.

brought from their home or hospital to the funeral home), how to dress caskets, attend to the paperwork, and many of the huge number of tasks that make up the funeral director's job. I was able to engage with the families of the deceased. I really wanted to give my all to those families and take care of them properly.

Our family moved to Mount Wellington to be closer to my work and our new home was a lovely older house. It was a big improvement over Manurewa, even though there was no insulation and sometimes water would be running down the walls inside. We bought two dehumidifiers and kept them running all the time, but it seemed the kids – by now we had Moronai as well – were always getting sick. Somehow life was good, though.

In the early days, Kaiora really struggled with what I was doing. She didn't like the fact that I was coming home wearing the same clothes that I had been wearing around dead people all day, so she used to make me take them off and leave them in the garage before I came into the house. Once, when I had to bring the removal car home – even though there wasn't a body in it – she made me park it far from the house. She was worried that the wairua of people who had been in it would still be around. I think she would have liked me to shower with holy water too before I came inside.

I tried to talk to her about my work, partly because that's what husbands and wives are supposed to do, but also because I needed to unload some of the emotion that built up with the job every day. I could only share my interactions with families and their grief, not so much my interactions with the deceased and the work I did with them, as my wife wasn't quite ready to hear about it. None of my whānau wanted to hear about it either.

At family functions, everyone would get to tell their work stories.

'I've got a work story,' I'd say. 'Today, I —'

'No, thank you, Francis, no one wants to hear those kinds of stories. We're trying to have a nice time here.'

I don't really know what my whānau thought about me becoming a funeral director when there was no family tradition of it. They never asked. They knew I was following my dream, and I think a few of them might have been waiting for me to decide I had had enough and go back to a proper job, once I had got it out of my system.

But it wasn't like that.

Also, Māori funeral needs weren't being met well by traditional funeral directors. I liked Lagoon View because that was their kaupapa. Lagoon View was started by three Māori gentlemen. When I joined, Ramsey Joyce, one of the original founders, was in charge. I still didn't have any professional qualifications – and I wouldn't become a qualified funeral director for quite a while. I was too busy learning on the job to do any study.

EVENTUALLY THE TIME felt right to take the plunge and go to work for myself. I was twenty-three. I had always looked up to the big firms like Davis Funerals and Morrisons, but I wanted to serve the Māori and Pacific Island communities. My wife and I were part of setting up Waitakere Funerals in west Auckland with an older friend and his wife.

Today, Kaiora is as much a part of Tipene Funerals as I am, but she wasn't keen at the start. It was never her passion and I had to draw her into it. But because of the sort of good person she is, I knew it wouldn't take much.

Although she didn't like to talk about it at first, gradually I encouraged her to share my interest. Once I had a coroner's case which involved a young woman who was the same age as Kaiora. She had died at Middlemore Hospital while she was in labour but before she had had the baby. It was a very sad case and when I told my wife about it she was interested because it really touched her heart.

That led to us talking more about the job and the what-ifs of life. It felt close to us because of the experience Kaiora had had giving birth to Nikora.

At that point, she got the emotional connection that makes being a funeral director much more than just a job.

So from then on, when I got home from work and she asked how I was, I would say, 'Okay,' but then just start talking about the experiences I had had in the day, especially the tragedies that reminded me why we do what we do.

One day, I was dressing a body on my own and needed help. There was no one else around so I rang Kaiora at home.

'Sweetheart, can you put the boys in the car and come up and help me with this lady?' I said.

'Are you for real?'

'There's no one else here. I just need help moving a body.'

The woman was quite big. Her family wanted me to dress her but didn't want to help themselves.

'All right, I'm coming.'

So Kaiora came up with the babies. Our home was only a couple of kilometres from the funeral home, but she was so reluctant she managed to make the drive take ten minutes at least. It took her that long to prepare herself mentally, even though she had been around death before and it should have been fine.

Eventually she arrived and put the children down in another room and joined me. I introduced her to the deceased woman.

'Drag her wrist and roll her this way,' I told her, and she did it without a worry.

I was so happy when I saw how she was acting. She was just naturally talking to the old lady, telling her what was going to happen.

'Dear, I'm just going to take your wrist and help my husband dress you.'

The human element was there, and I hadn't had to tell her anything. She kept talking to the old lady. I talked to her too. And Kaiora and I talked to each other. She even told me not to be too rough. After all, except for our children, we don't usually dress other human beings. Sometimes with a body, you have to pull quite hard, but Kaiora wanted me to be gentle.

Then it was all over and the woman was in the casket. Kaiora was still there when the family came in.

'My mum looks so beautiful – thank you so much,' they told her, and she told me later she instantly got a feeling for the work.

Then there were more cases where I needed her to help and she just drifted into it and it became part of her. I didn't really notice it happening, then suddenly there she was, a natural funeral director.

OF COURSE, NO ONE had heard of me, and the name Waitakere Funerals didn't mean anything to anyone. We didn't have any money to spend on advertising, so I had to come up with some way of getting us known that wouldn't cost anything.

At that time, there was a programme on Māori TV called *Homai te Pakipaki.* It was basically a karaoke show on TV. There were ten contestants each week and the person who won got a thousand dollars and went to the next round. The overall winner won $10,000. I had always watched the show, which had a big mainstream following as well as a Māori audience. But I never dreamt I would end up performing on it.

'You should do this,' said Kaiora.

Apart from kapa haka and singing at funerals, which was something I had always done, I hadn't really sung in public before. Certainly not like a regular entertainer. But I could see this was a great opportunity to get my name out there, so I gave in and we went down to the auditions at the Māori TV studios. They were held on Friday afternoon and the live show was later the same night.

On the way, I was practising and trying to decide what song to sing, but when I got there, they gave me a list to choose from. Once I saw 'How Can You Mend a Broken Heart?' I knew that was the right song for me. I was lucky enough to be chosen to go in the live broadcast.

I went in hoping to win but never thought I would. There were some beautiful singers among the other contestants. Viewers text votes for their favourites, and that's how the winner is chosen.

I don't know how I won that night. Maybe it was what I did in the interview when I had to introduce myself in the get-to-know-the-contestant part of the show.

'My name is Francis and I'm a singing funeral director.'

'Francis, if you won the $10,000, what would you spend it on?'

'I'd buy some new wheels for my hearse.'

Then I sang my song and must have pulled a few heartstrings because my name was read out at the end.

I sang 'Save the Last Dance for Me' at the semis and qualified with four others to sing live at the grand final, held before a big audience at the Logan Campbell Centre. I didn't win that, but I came second.

And it worked, because as well as the exposure I got with the TV audience, the suburban newspaper that covered the area our business was aimed at did a story on me. Naturally, the headline was 'Dead Certainty for Final'. So far as anyone knows, I'm the first funeral director in the world to have based their marketing on a TV talent show.

Nan was over the moon. I know she's proud of me but she's a quiet person when it comes to handing out praise.

She rang me when the show had been on: 'Oh, you won. That's good. When are you on next? I'll let you go now. Okay, bye.'

That's heaps coming from her.

THINGS DIDN'T GO WELL with the partnership at Waitakere Funerals. We parted company and then Kaiora and I set up Tipene Funerals in Henderson in 2013 and in Onehunga two years later.

This was a big leap for us. At Waitakere Funerals, my partner and his wife were vastly more experienced in business than me and Kaiora, so we could rely on them a lot.

It was different when it was just the two of us. Then the pressure was really on, because it was unheard of for a young Māori couple to be doing this. In fact, in both my family and hers, it was unheard of for anyone to have any kind of business.

There was some pride involved. We wanted to prove something to ourselves and we also wanted to make our families proud.

Finance was always a worry. Our payment terms were thirty days and we hoped and prayed people would pay on time so we could survive. We did about a dozen funerals a month if we were lucky, but that was enough to keep us going with the help of our assistant, Tyrone.

He was a good friend who had the same values and principles as us, plus a strong work ethic. But, also, he was deeply entrenched in this tikanga, which was what we needed. Māori people were our market.

Starting a funeral business is expensive. We didn't need to have a mortuary, as Auckland is lucky to have a very good freelance embalmer, Rikki Solomon, who does that job for smaller firms who don't have their own facilities.

But you need stock in the form of caskets; and hearses are specialist vehicles. And everything in your reception lounge and visiting rooms and offices has to be super presentable.

We bought everything from Trade Me. We couldn't afford brand-new hearses, but we bought beautiful old cars and converted them for funerals and made them look good. Even now, except for our computers, we never buy anything brand-new; it's all second-hand. Our cars aren't always in the best condition when we get them, much to my wife's dismay.

My first hearse at Tipene Funerals was a 1999 silver Cadillac purchased from Robert J Cotton and Sons, funeral directors in Palmerston North. I loved it. I drove around with it empty sometimes because it was so beautiful. It did many funerals and turned a lot of heads and was the pride and joy of the fleet. I've still got it.

In the early days, we decorated the funeral home with furniture from our own home. So Kaiora and I went without at home for a while, but we knew we had to do it. We wanted the funeral homes to be welcoming and comfortable for families waiting for their loved ones to be prepared.

Once we started doing what we loved for ourselves, everything started to flow. Of course, it had an impact on our home life. We were putting everything into the business, and the children had to fit around that. We lived on takeaways because there was never enough time to cook a meal.

They were hard times. We just put our heads down and prayed there would be light at the end of the tunnel.

I was in my early thirties and never thought about my own mortality. This business was something I really wanted to do and back then I just kept going and dragged everyone along with me. But looking back, and knowing what I know now about how quickly death can strike without warning, I wonder if it was the best way to be. I gradually realised I needed to balance my own life between work and family.

Funeral directors do have a different perspective on death from most people. A lot of our work is with people who have died too young, in their thirties and forties, whether from accidents or diseases such as cancer. Some are slow deaths and some are sudden. Some are people we have known ourselves. Some are young mums and dads with babies and toddlers.

There was one thing we did differently from other funeral directors that I think helped not just our work–life balance but

The headline was
'Dead Certainty for Final'.
So far as anyone knows,
I'm the first funeral
director in the world to
have based their marketing
on a TV talent show.

also the grieving families we dealt with: we always included our young children in our work. To be honest, we had no choice, because with us both doing the funerals, the kids just had to tag along and be part of things.

This began with Mikae, who was born in 2013 when we were running the funeral home in Henderson by ourselves.

'I'm Francis. This is my wife, Kaiora,' I said when people came through the door. 'Welcome to our family funeral home. This is our pēpi.'

Kaiora might have had a baby in her arms when a grieving family came to arrange a funeral or spend time with their loved one. She just introduced Mikae at the same time as she introduced herself.

And people really liked it. I think babies make you feel good. Often the family asked to hold the baby and then they passed him around among themselves. It took their minds off things and somehow I think the new life put the one that had gone in perspective.

'He's so lovely … Can we give him his bottle? … Is it okay if we change him?'

Sometimes people objected when Kaiora was pregnant. Not because she was tapu or anything like that, but because they were worried about her doing any heavy lifting of caskets or bodies.

The only time it got a bit difficult – and actually this happened quite a few times – was when we were at home with the kids and the work phone came through with someone wanting to arrange a funeral, and the moment I answered it the baby started crying. Then there'd be a hang-up so I'd have to call back the number on my phone.

'Hello – I just missed a call from this number …'

'Oh yes, that was me. I was trying to call the funeral director but I heard a baby crying.'

'No, you've got the right number. Sorry about that …'

I think being Māori made this all seem more natural. We didn't try to work out beforehand whether people would be open to having a baby around when they were talking about organising a tangi. For Māori, everything is about family. We had positioned ourselves as a Māori funeral home, so people knew that we would be family-oriented.

Henderson was a natural place to start a funeral home with an emphasis on serving Māori and Pacific Island families, because there was no one offering this service to people out that way. When I was at Lagoon View in Panmure, we did many Māori funerals from Henderson even though it was nearly thirty kilometres across town. So we started there, where there was an established Māori community needing a funeral director.

Things grew steadily. I feel a great sense of honour that so many people trusted us. The business we have now is something I would only have dared dream about when I was starting out.

I ask myself sometimes – between the dead and the living, where is the line or boundary? It's all part of the marae and home for Māori. In our chapel, there is more laughter than crying, which is so beautiful.

'Manawa mai e! Tatau mai e!'

———————

An ancient Ngāpuhi incantation to remove tapu

CHAPTER FIVE

YOUR TOP FIVE QUESTIONS

I SPEND A FAIR BIT OF TIME breaking down prejudices about funerals and funeral directors. Or maybe I should say I used to, because I have a TV programme that's done it for me. And now I have a book.

I don't think I'm a stereotypical funeral director. I'm certainly young to have my own firm. A lot of people say, 'I didn't realise how normal you are.'

When you become a funeral director, you have to deal with lots of challenges: families' tragedies, long and uncivilised hours, sometimes grisly physical situations. And people's questions. Lots and lots of questions.

When I first started, if my family showed any interest at all, it mainly came down to one question: 'Oh, cuz, how could you do that?'

I understood. I came from the same background as they did. When we thought about death, it was about the sacredness of it and how tapu it was. They thought funeral directing was all about ghosts and spirits, not bodies and paperwork.

That didn't faze me at all. It was a conversation we had to have.

But I didn't realise I was going to have to have it with everyone I met. Once people found out what I did, they didn't want to talk about anything else. Beforehand, I thought it would be a conversation stopper, but really it was a conversation starter. Death is one mystery, funerals are another, and people are naturally curious about things that are so important and that will happen to them one day. They want to find out as much as they can, when they get the chance.

That was fine for a while. Then I started to lie so I didn't have to talk about it, because I got sick of hearing myself saying the same thing over and over again.

I imagine it is much the same for police officers: 'How many people have you arrested? Has anyone ever tried to shoot you?' Actually, I'd love to sit down with a police officer for a while and hear about what they go through.

Sometimes I said I worked at The Warehouse, which in a funny way was a genuine fantasy of mine. I wouldn't mind a job where I got to talk to lots of different people all day. And I've always been fascinated by how the checkout works. When I was a kid, I was even fascinated by the ding that sounded every time something got scanned.

That noise had a special significance for me. When we went to Kaitaia to do our shopping on benefit day and I was waiting in line with Nan and Pop, every time that ding sounded it meant something else was coming home to Pawarenga with us. When

I go shopping now, I use the self-checkout, so I can make the ding noise myself.

Just when I thought I could stop talking about funerals, *The Casketeers* came along and got everyone interested again. I understand. I always reflect back on the burning desire I had, when I was thinking about entering the industry, to know about what happens behind those closed doors.

But the TV show means that since 2018 I haven't been able to get away with my story about The Warehouse. And I don't need to tell people as much about what I do, either – they've seen it on TV. They are not shy about approaching me and they always say they love the show, which is nice, but then the questions start again.

So here for anyone who is curious are my Top Five Questions I Get Asked About Funeral Directing.

1. Is it scary?

Yes. Well, it is to me. That's why I always leave the lights on.

For Māori, the time the spirits come alive to cross over is in the early hours of the morning. Some people believe it happens at the time of death, others believe it is at the time of the tangi.

Hine-Nui-te-Pō is the goddess of both night and death. I can't do anything about the death, but I can do something about the night. If you ever drive past one of our funeral homes at night, there are lights on all over the building, and I don't care about power bills. They are all LED, of course.

If it is night time and I have been called out to uplift a body, I don't want to have to walk into a dark building. I want to be able to see where I am going when I go in to collect the stretcher. So we turn off the big house lights but leave lamps on all through the building. It doesn't matter where you are, you will still be able to see, and there are no dark corners. The lamp shops love me. They are always happy when I walk in.

It's not just for me. I have staff with similar backgrounds and traditions who also believe spirits are active in the dark. So I keep the lights on for them too.

I realise this is ironic and, besides any religious element, probably has a deep psychological aspect to it. After all, I grew up in a home with no electricity, and here I am keeping as many lights on as I can.

It's not all about superstition. I just really want to see if there is anything there. One night at 1 am, I had a removal. We had just leased a new building to keep our cars and caskets in, and when I got there to pick up a car, all the lights were off. I opened the door and it was pitch black. I hate that. I hate the idea there could be something there I don't know about and can't see. It was freaky.

I used the torch on my phone to find a light switch and disabled the alarm. When all the lights came on, I could see the removal car and realised there was obviously nothing to worry about. And of course, I knew there was nothing to worry about right from the start. But it was a new building, I couldn't see anything and I didn't know what was there. It wasn't even a funeral home – just a glorified garage and storeroom. There were no dead bodies there.

But I got that feeling. And once you get it, it's impossible to get rid of.

This has carried over to the rest of life, and even now that we're not living above the business any more, which we were for

When I'm driving at night and I have a casket with a body in it in the back of the car, I tilt the mirror so I can't see the lid. Just in case. It would be awful if it moved.

a few years, I still have to have all the lights on at home. Again, all LED, of course.

So I am … cautious about the dark, but I've never been scared of being around the dead. Well, that's not exactly true.

One night, in my early funeral directing days, one of my former employers left me with a body in a mortuary. It was a no-view body, which meant the family weren't expected to come to visit. So, although it would still be treated with respect, how we made it look wasn't quite so important.

'Can you tidy it up anyway?' said my boss, because it was the right thing to do. 'Do the hair, close the eyes. Do a little embalming – raise the vessels and the veins.' I had been taught a few basics of embalming on the job. I hadn't done a course, but I could do that much.

This was at 10.30 at night. It was dark out and I was by myself in the mortuary. I thought I would be all right. I turned the radio on for company. I ran a tap. I started singing. I did everything I could think of, but nothing worked. It was the first time I'd been completely alone with a dead body. And it was late. In that big empty building. With all those noises. I couldn't handle it.

I took my gear off, walked out of the mortuary and texted my boss: 'I'm sorry. I can't do it.'

'What's wrong?'

I had to tell him the truth. I was too scared to stay there. I felt there were ghosts and spirits around and once that idea gets in your head you can't shift it. He wasn't very impressed but there was nothing he could do about it.

And yes, even to this day, I can still get scared. The difference now is that because I run the business I can't give in to it. Otherwise a lot of people won't get paid. I force myself to keep going.

I know it's silly. I know nothing can happen. But still, when I'm driving at night and I have a casket with a body in it in the back of the car, I tilt the mirror so I can't see the lid. Just in case. It would be awful if it moved.

2. What about spirits?

I don't feel them as such, but I know they are around. There are times when I might be with a body and I'm joking, or being rude to myself or the staff, or we are playing around and the person who is dead doesn't like it, and things happen.

The problem might occur later on. Something goes wrong and I realise it's the dead person making their feelings known. So I apologise. That is why we always do the work as if the person is still alive: *Would I say this in front of her?*

Kaiora has always been like that. If I'm in the dressing room with a body, she doesn't just walk in. She knocks first.

'Francis, can I see you outside?'

'I'm just doing a body – can you tell me now?'

'No, I can't.'

So we go outside and talk so the dead person won't hear.

Sometimes, if I've done something wrong, a body plays up and won't behave the way I want it to. For instance, when I was a much bigger boy than I am now, doing a removal of an overweight body was a substantial challenge for me. I might let my feelings be known as I huffed and puffed to get the body into the car.

'I wish you hadn't had that last Big Mac,' I might say to the body. 'And I think you ate too many pies.'

And then the body would start purging when it was being embalmed, and I knew that was his way of saying, 'I didn't like your rude comments. Don't talk like that to me. And you should take a look at how many pies you have been eating.'

Once, I had picked up a lady from hospital and her family were rude and mean.

'Gee, your family are a real pack of mongrels,' I told her. 'How did you put up with them?'

And when I was trying to embalm her, everything went wrong and I knew it was because of what I had said. I apologised: 'I'm sorry for what I said about your family. I am sure they are very nice people really. They are your whānau, after all. I forgot they are grieving and not their usual selves.' And after that everything went okay.

3. Do bodies make noises?

I never knew what people meant when they asked me this. It's not something I thought about when I wasn't a funeral director, but apparently it's on a lot of people's minds.

And the answer is no – most of the time. But sometimes you might hear a noise from the back of the removal vehicle when you are transporting a body. If you have put the strap on too tight around the tummy, it will push a little air out and you'll hear a sort of gurgle-groan noise.

The first time I heard it, I stopped the car and rang my boss.

'I know I have a death certificate here,' I said, 'but I don't think this body is dead.'

'Get out and have a look.'

He stayed on the phone while I opened the side door. It looked dead.

'How tight have you got the straps?'

'Really tight. I didn't want it to move around.'

'It's just the straps pushing on the stomach. It's nothing to worry about.'

So now I make sure I don't put the straps on too tight. And just to confirm: dead people don't make a sound.

You read stories about it from overseas sometimes but, although it is a basic fear, it's very rare for a live person to be mistaken for dead.

I also worry a fair bit about back doors on vehicles coming open and caskets rolling out and away, but that's not really a fear. That's more worry about doing the job right. That's why we have good strong clips to keep caskets and stretchers in place.

4. What's the scariest or craziest thing that's ever happened to you at work?

That's easy. Something really terrifying happened to us once, and we still don't know what it was.

When we moved into our building in Onehunga, where the funeral home was downstairs and the Tipene home was upstairs, we hadn't had a proper blessing of the premises. We were doing renovations at the same time and just hadn't got around to organising the ceremony. Before we took over, the whole place had been a funeral home.

We moved in about a week before the official opening was due to take place. That was also when we were going to get around to having the karakia and the blessing. And on that first night, when we were all there together and just having an ordinary quiet night at home, suddenly there was the most tremendous bang.

'Did you hear that?' I asked Kaiora.

'Yep.' It would have been impossible for her to miss it.

And then it came again.

I went to investigate with my torches. I was wearing a head-light torch and had a regular torch in each hand. Some of the lights were off, so I went right around the building and turned every light on.

I made it down the back of the funeral home part of the building and suddenly, right in front of my face, there was the same loud bang again.

I wondered where the hell it was. I know it sounded right in front of me, but there was nothing there. So now, even though I had all the lights on, I was scared.

'Honey!' I called, and Kaiora came running.

'What have we done wrong?' I said. 'Who have we offended that is angry with us?'

We stayed there for ages, poking around and looking for something that might have made the noise, but we couldn't find anything. I looked in the roof, but couldn't find anything there. It didn't happen again and eventually we went to bed. We slept very badly that night.

The next day I was determined to find the logical explanation – there had to be one. Maybe it was something electrical in the roof? I called an electrician in. And a builder in case it was something to do with that. Neither of them could find anything wrong. So I just put it down to someone being silly.

That night we were a lot more relaxed and settling down for a pleasant evening when, all of a sudden, out of nowhere, once again came that terrible bang.

We were ready to go to a hotel. We were absolutely petrified. But we couldn't panic or react too much because we didn't want to scare the kids.

Then it happened again. It was so loud, but at the same time you couldn't say it was in one corner or another corner; it seemed to be in the middle of everything. We both freaked out.

It was so loud I was sure the neighbours must have heard. I went to the people down the back.

'Sorry to bother you. Did you hear a loud bang from our place just before?'

'No. We didn't hear a thing.'

Then I went to the neighbours on the side.

'Sorry to bother you. Did you hear a loud bang from our place just before?'

'Sorry – no, we didn't.'

Kaiora and I looked and looked. We didn't tell the children anything. When they asked about the noise, we just said there was some building going on next door.

I was sure I hadn't done anything wrong to annoy or offend one of the dead people who were under our roof those nights.

I know that the last funeral company that had occupied the building had stored ashes in the part of the building that we had made our sleeping quarters. Those ashes hadn't been claimed by their whānau and because many of them had been kept there for years, it had been impossible for our predecessors to track down next of kin. The liquidators of the previous company had had to dispose of them. By the time we took over, they were gone.

Preparing the body and decorating the caskets and the showy stuff are an important part of the job, but one of the main things to remember about funerals is that they are for the living, not the dead.

That all came to mind over this incident, but with our faith and spiritual values we weren't moved. And we didn't think we had done anything to upset anyone.

We rang our staff and told them the problem. When they came in to work, they could see what a bad state we were in. But they pointed out we hadn't had the karakia and the blessing.

Of course. How could I have been so dumb?

So, after two nearly sleepless nights, we decided to bring the blessing forward and get it over with. A priest came and performed the ceremony and from that point we never had a problem.

And that was the scariest thing that has happened in my career, mainly because we didn't know what was happening, and we still don't know. At least if a body sat up in a casket and started talking to you, you would know where the noise came from.

5. Why do you do it?

My choice of funeral directing as a profession has something to do with leadership, I think. There are prominent leaders such as prime ministers and presidents, but there are also people who lead in other ways.

From an early age, at my school up north, I was always told to stand up on the taumata to welcome the manuhiri and do the mihi. I had to lead that performance. It was not something I asked for; it was something the teachers told me to do, so I did it. And it was not a case of being sent to sit down and learn from this kaumātua or that kuia. I just had to learn by doing it.

'Francis, get up there.' And I got up there. They must have seen some potential or leadership skills in me, so they pushed me forward. It was not something I sought out.

Before I got into funeral directing, I wanted to be a bus driver. That involves leading people from the front and taking them with you. Now I am in a business where I also lead people – in funeral processions.

Preparing the body and decorating the caskets and the showy stuff are an important part of the job, but one of the main things to remember about funerals is that they are for the living, not the dead. A funeral director leads the living on a journey of loss. A funeral procession is like a massive bus, with the hearse in front and the mourners as the passengers in the cars following behind.

I don't know if it says something about my ego or the sort of person I am, but I feel comfortable out there in front of the funeral, just like I did in front of the people on the marae.

Of course, I could have stuck to my original plan and led people by sitting at the front of a bus and taking them wherever they wanted to go. But I didn't, so the question to ask is really why I chose to lead funerals not passengers.

The conclusion I have come to is that after attending all those tangi at school and work, I felt naturally drawn to them because they involved so much of our culture and tikanga – as well as the out-the-front stuff.

When I was growing up, all the funerals I attended were on the marae. When I got into the industry, that was the only kind of funeral I knew about. The marae is like a wānanga for me. That is where I got most of my real education. So I thought, *Let's do funerals for a living, because it is vital work and they will use everything I have learnt growing up in terms of tangihanga, te reo Māori and te ao Māori.*

E kore e hohoro te opeope o te otaota

An important task is not completed in haste

CHAPTER SIX

THE CARE
OF THE LIVING

THERE ARE TWO main kinds of people I work with – the living and the dead. The living are much more demanding. But the customer is always right, even in funerals, and we as an industry are constantly adapting.

A recent trend is for the family to have a longer gap between the death and the funeral. A few decades ago this was always three days, unless there were very special circumstances. It probably dates back to the era before modern embalming when there was a need to dispose of the body quickly for health reasons.

Today, a lot of Māori and Pasifika families need more time to prepare because many of their members might have moved to Australia or be coming back from Tonga or Samoa.

When my grandfather died in January 2018, we had to take that into account. We worked out the plan in advance. Whether he died in Auckland or up north, his body would be prepared in Auckland and kept there until the whānau from the South Island and overseas had time to get back from wherever they were. Then we would all drive him up north together. Everything went according to plan. Until his unveiling, that is, but I'll get to that later.

People who want alternatives to traditional funerals are likely to look for alternatives to traditional funeral directors. I know a lot of the big funeral directors work very hard to give people what they want these days. For the ones in the middle, like us, it's a bit harder because they may not have the resources to deviate too much from the norm. But in our case, we have always had a reputation for being different anyway, with our focus on Māori and Pasifika farewells.

We start with providing the basics – what needs to happen for legal and practical reasons – and then go on to find out what people want to happen, and try to do as much of that as possible.

Personally, I like a lot of the old-fashioned ways of doing things. The ceremony in Catholic funerals, for instance, is very beautiful to me. It is so structured, and every part is full of meaning and tradition. I love it when I'm not directly involved and can just sit back and watch the priest performing his different actions, especially at the end with the thurible and the incense. Best of all is when a funeral is being held at St Patrick's Cathedral in the centre of Auckland. That's such a beautiful building and the atmosphere adds a lot to the ceremony.

That's not to say I prefer Catholic beliefs to those of other religions – I'm still a Mormon, after all. At Mormon funerals, there is not a lot that is prescribed. They are very personal and people speak from the heart. I just like the way Catholics do things.

The only time I get really nervous during a funeral is when I have to be on duty at a requiem mass, because that adds to the number of things that can go wrong – which is high enough to start with.

Sometimes there will be an altar boy or altar girl to assist the priest during the mass. But if there isn't, then that job goes to me. I have to lock the thurible to keep everything in place when the incense is lit at the end of the service. Altar boys and girls probably have it completely sussed, but I'm never sure exactly when I should be lighting the incense in order to spread the sweet-smelling scent but not smoke the building out.

In an ideal world, it would stay alight. Sometimes it goes out and nothing happens. Sometimes there is too much smoke. It's stressful.

Catholic Māori funerals are the best of both worlds for me. I don't know a lot of Pākehā hymns, but I know all the Māori ones, so I can join in and sing to honour the person being farewelled.

When families have the time to sit with us and organise photos to be printed on a casket or have their favourite flower, or their motorbike or fishing rod or fish put on it, we can usually do that. But for a lot of families it's about how little time they have. That is why pre-arranging funerals is amazing. We hold some beautiful caskets that have elaborate designs, but personalising them comes at a cost.

HUMOUR IS A LARGE PART of our daily life and our business. And sometimes even at funerals too. The days when it was forbidden to smile or laugh at a funeral are long gone. People often say, when they are arranging the funeral or at the start of the service, that they don't want any tears because this guy was a real joker and just so funny.

And those funerals often end up being the saddest.

Perhaps it's because people who have spent their days making their mates laugh have been doing it to make up for something really sad in their lives. At these funerals, people get up and go on about the jokes and crack-up times. Then someone will stand up and say, 'I'll tell you about a side of Dad you didn't know,' and there will be a really poignant moment. The funniness has gone and everyone understands the sadness behind it all.

I like to make people laugh, but it's not part of my job to make the jokes. At the same time, I can use it to lighten the mood or put people at ease.

It depends on the situation, but often it will be when a family has come in to arrange a funeral. The joke will never be about the funeral or the deceased. It is more likely to be a joke on me. And that breaks the ice and makes it easier for the people to open up and let their feelings out a bit. Making that happen is part of the funeral director's job.

When I started, I was so serious. I didn't dare to laugh or risk offending anyone. Then I saw another funeral director working – an older woman called Tania, who had the knack. She was hilarious. You liked her or you didn't, but most people loved her. They rang up and asked for Tania because they had heard about her from their friends.

She was letting her personality show, and I realised if you can be yourself, things will work a lot better. You can share your own experiences (but never your opinions).

She made me see that being a funeral director didn't mean you had to be a robot. I was being a robot. A lot of funeral directors appear like robots, but people need to know funeral directors are sympathetic and understanding. It's a fine line. It's easy to appear cold and impersonal but what we are really doing is keeping things under control so people can go through their own experience of grief.

THIS FUNERAL BUSINESS has always had unfriendly hours. Unfortunately, people do not die between nine in the morning and five in the afternoon. Even between eight and six would be good. But we are expected to work – and we do expect to work – around the clock. If someone has just suffered a bereavement, they want their loved one taken care of straight away, not left to go stiff and cold all alone. We have to be ready to drop everything and go out at any time of the day or night.

We have a roster for our staff and everyone shares the load. About once a month everyone has a turn answering the phone. Pardon the cliché, but this is a people business – and when people get in contact, they want to be in contact with a person. They don't want to have to leave their details to be called back later, or put through to an answering service that will pass a message on.

That can be a nightmare if it's a busy night. It is very intrusive on your family and home life.

People have tried to sell me alternatives but I can't bring myself to do it. So my cellphone number is out there for anyone who wants to ring me. If I don't pick up, it defaults to the next person on the roster, and if they don't pick up, it goes to the next person and so on. Whatever happens, a person who might be dealing with the first stages of grief will get to speak to a sympathetic human at the other end of the phone.

The staff understand this. In fact, I think I complain about having to answer the phone more than they do. That's because since *The Casketeers* so many people want to talk about the show. 'Is it really you?' they say and can get completely side-tracked. They want to talk about the cars or the leaf blower or anything else you can imagine, instead of what to do about Mum or Uncle. And all I want to do is go back to sleep.

On a more positive note, I appreciate how often people say that the Francis and Kaiora they meet in real life are just like the couple they see on the programme.

THE OTHER THING people are saying more and more often when it comes to arranging a funeral is that they 'just want something really simple'. This might be because it's what their loved one wanted, or it might be because it's what their whānau have decided they would have wanted.

The problem is that everyone has a different idea of what 'simple' means. I might think it means one thing, and the family might think it means another, and Mum might have thought it meant a third – but she's not here and didn't leave instructions, so we will never know.

The immediate family arranging the funeral might ask for six red roses on a plain casket, one viewing at the funeral home and a half-hour service. But when word gets out to others, everything can change. It's often the deceased's siblings versus their children, and they will start putting their oar in.

'I'd like to have some chrysanthemums on the casket too. She always loved chrysanthemums when we were growing up.'

'My son can't get up from Dunedin till tomorrow so we'd like to arrange an extra viewing in the afternoon.'

People get up and go
on about the jokes and
crack-up times. Then
someone will stand up
and say, 'I'll tell you about
a side of Dad you didn't
know,' and there will be
a really poignant moment.

'Some of Mum's friends from work and bridge want to say a few words, so we'll probably need to make the service an hour.'

That's all fine. Funerals are for the living.

On one occasion, a family said they just wanted a drop-off at the crematorium. This is popular with people who really, really don't want a funeral service. It's a funeral without the service. We just drop the body off at the crematorium. The staff cremate it and later we pick up the ashes, and then the family – usually – collects them. This is for those people who have said: 'Just burn me and get rid of the ashes somewhere.' Which might be fine for them. But funerals are for the living.

For this drop-off, the family decided at the last minute to follow me to the crematorium. Then we got there and predictably – and understandably – they wanted to have a few moments with their loved one before she was cremated. I have been known to change my mind sometimes too; I wasn't going to argue with them.

For many people, the chance to go to war over what the funeral arrangements should be is their one last stand in family feuds that may have been raging since they were children. It's now or never for getting your own way over something. The funeral director is definitely in the middle, and if I had my time over again I'd try to study for some sort of psychology/family feud/conflict resolution degree if one exists. If it doesn't, someone should invent one. It would make my job a lot easier.

I had another drop-off that was very complicated. The man didn't have a wife or children. His sister made the arrangements, and as far as she was concerned, the simpler the better. She asked us to uplift the body from the rest home and take it straight to the crematorium and she would pick up the ashes the next day.

It sounded like a simple plan, but just as I was about to leave for the rest home, the phone rang.

It was a woman who worked with the deceased at the school where he had once taught, and she had just heard about his demise.

'Can you tell us when the service would be? There's quite a few of us from school who would like to come and pay our respects.'

That was awkward. I was definitely in two minds. The sister was the person instructing me – and paying me. On the other hand, these sounded like nice people and it appeared the man had a lot of connections in this community.

Sometimes there is a hard choice between what someone wants and what is right.

The woman was shocked when I told her what was happening.

'Really – you mean to tell me there's no service?'

'Dear, I'm literally ten minutes away from taking him to the crematorium,' I explained. 'If you call his sister, she'll explain a bit more.'

'There's no need,' said the woman and she hung up. She sounded angry and disappointed. I was torn but it wasn't my call.

To be candid, from a business point of view, when someone has a simple funeral we lose revenue opportunities on all sorts of things: the chapel, a reception venue, catering, cars, flowers and a lot more. That's a commercial reality.

But to me, the much more important reason to have a funeral is that people want to pay their respects and this gives everyone a chance to do that and start to deal with their loss. If I didn't believe it was important to have dignified, appropriate funerals for people, I'd be driving a bus. Much less stressful.

You don't need flowers –
most people bring them
anyway. You don't need
catering – get people
to bring a plate back
to a relative's house.
You don't need a fleet
of mourning cars.

Funerals don't need to be expensive. People can choose lower-price options at every level and keep everyone happy, including the person paying the bills. You don't need flowers – most people bring them anyway. You don't need catering – get people to bring a plate back to a relative's house. You don't need a fleet of mourning cars – just one big enough to fit the casket. I would rather talk my business out of a fee than see someone go without a funeral because of money worries.

These days, people still stick to the traditional options when they are planning or arranging funerals. Doves and balloons that get released into the sky are pretty standard accessories. They're a beautiful symbol for letting someone go emotionally, or to represent their departure from this world.

People sometimes ask if it is all right to wear bright colours to lighten the mood. And I say, of course, and we will wear something bright too. But that will just be a tie or small item, because there is a good chance the people will turn up in dark colours after all, and you don't want the funeral director to be the only one there in a canary-yellow suit.

There is another part of looking after the living that we never charge for and which often goes unnoticed. In fact, if we do it properly it won't be noticed. It is that we carry grief for people. I can see why sometimes people think we are a bit emotionless. It's because we keep our emotions under control to keep proceedings on track. That means the mourners don't have to worry about practicalities and can let their emotions out.

I find this a very hard part of the job because I'm an emotional person. No matter how hard I try not to let my emotions show, they often get the better of me. I feel bad because it's my job not to let my feelings out.

My tie often doubles as a tissue if I need to mop up a tear or two. Silk ones are no good because they aren't absorbent, so I always wear cotton to funerals. Using a tie helps me be discreet if I shed a tear. I'm not pulling out a hankie and waving it around.

Actually, I should make the point that it's not a good idea to wipe your eyes with a tie because when you're picking up or dressing bodies, the end of your tie touches the body all the time. It may not be very hygienic.

If I know I'm going to be a real mess at a service, I get busy to distract myself. I give the flowers a bit of a spruce up. Or I pop out and check the car is okay. Or I find tissues for mourners, but I'm actually doing it for myself. I take the first one, then pass the box around.

Emotional moments can occur anywhere, any time. One that left a lasting impression on me was a cremation. The woman's grown children did not want to view the charge – which is when mourners get one last look at the casket before it goes into the cremator. But her adult grandchildren did.

I explained to them what would happen: the curtains are closed when the family go in so they can't see the cremator being prepared, the curtain will open, the cremator door will rise, Nan in her casket will be placed into it quickly and then the door will come down.

When the curtain went up and they saw their grandmother's casket on the trolley about to be pushed in the cremator, their cries got louder. First, it was a low moan. Then the door went up and they started to wail. That had me in tears. Then it got even louder. I thought: *I can't watch this; you guys make me so sad.* It's not the action of the cremation, it's the reaction of the family that gets to your heart.

This same thing happened with Fiona, who works with us, when her dad was cremated. I know her so well. We have done so many funerals together and I had seen her shed tears before. But when it was her dad she was crying for, I felt so sad I couldn't bear to watch her.

I can't say it enough: funeral directors need to have big hearts and leave them open.

It's easy to lose touch of the emotional side when you spend so much of your time organising finance and flowers and dealing with council staff and fretting about little details. When you actually own the business, you can lose your connection with why you got into it in the first place. That experience with the grandchildren and the cremation was very grounding for me. It brought me back to the starting point.

When I hear people talking about funerals giving 'closure', I always cringe a bit. I hate that word. Yes, life does go on without the person who died. For those who are left behind there is no choice about it and the world keeps turning.

But closure doesn't happen. People shouldn't expect to 'get over it', because they won't. A tutor for a course I once did explained it perfectly: there is never closure, there is moving on to the next stage of life. You can move forward with your own life but you will always have a gap where the person who you loved used to be. It's much easier to deal with death once you realise that. Then you don't expect some magic morning to wake up not feeling sad any more.

**I tuituia ai te mate hei kākahu mō te tangata, arā,
mō ngā mea hanga katoa**

———————————

**Death is woven as a shroud for all people
and, indeed, for all living things**

CHAPTER SEVEN

THE CARE OF THE DEAD

THE DEAD are much easier to deal with than the living, although they can reach out from beyond to make my life difficult.

We don't get too many requests that are out of the ordinary. Normally it's things like people wanting the funeral procession to drive past places that have been special to the person who has died, for one last look when they are on the way to the cemetery.

I had a funeral where I was asked not to make things too clean and tidy. If you know how much I obsess about cleanliness, you'll know how hard this was for me. The deceased was not into cleanliness at all, especially when it came to his car. I had made the arrangements and agreed to meet his whānau at Tipene Funerals the next morning. But they had one final request before I left.

'Could you not clean your car, please?' I was asked.

'Excuse me? My car?'

'He wouldn't like to be going anywhere in a clean car. Even dead.'

'Sorry – I don't think I understand.' Shiny clean cars are a basic part of our business. This didn't make any sense to me.

'Just go out and have a look at his car.'

I did, and it was filthy. Apparently, he never cleaned it. He was a 4WD nut who did lots of off-road stuff and just left his car dirty. There were a few gaps in the dirt where he had turned on the wipers so he could see through the windscreen, but that was it. Apparently, the only time it ever got cleaned properly was when he had to go for his warrant of fitness.

'But my car is black and if I don't clean it you will be able to see every bit of dirt,' I explained.

'Yeah, that's the point.'

I didn't clean the car, but it was a struggle. Fortunately, during the eulogy it was explained that the funeral director had left the hearse a bit dirty in keeping with the wishes of the deceased, so my reputation was saved.

The same man also had a rosewood coffin, which will show up any fingerprints if someone touches it. Normally we spray the casket to protect it and keep it pristine, but they asked us to leave that alone too, and by the time everything was over it was covered in fingerprints. They took photos of that.

I was mortified. When we were driving in procession, I kept an eye out to see if I was getting horrified looks from people as I drove past in my dirty hearse, but no one seemed bothered at all.

And that person got to have exactly the funeral he wanted to have. It was a bit difficult but I was glad to make the family happy. Although I certainly didn't put any of the pictures on my social media.

Once or twice a year, we organise a funeral for someone who comes to us from the City Mission who has no friends, family or even acquaintances who will attend their farewell and mourn for them.

It's very sad to think that someone's life has had so little impact on anyone else – or perhaps the wrong sort of impact, so they have been cut off from the people who might have loved them.

We do the basics for them. And then, depending on who is around, we will have a little prayer in the chapel ourselves. Any member of staff who would like to join in can do that. And whichever of the funeral directors is around will conduct the funeral. And if that is Fiona, who happens to be Samoan, then the person will get a Samoan hymn no matter if they are Pākehā or anything else.

Then we put the person in the car and take them to the crematorium. No one would ever know if we didn't do these things, but that is our job. Everyone deserves a little prayer and a send-off, and they get to have it in as good a hearse as anyone else.

Cars have always been a big part of the business. In fact, it's probably the second thing that comes to mind, after the casket, when people think about funerals and funeral directing.

I love the big American hearses. I'm not that interested in cars in general – just funeral cars. Most of all, I love our big black Cadillac – it's the one you see at the beginning of *The Casketeers*. It has a beautiful fake marble deck and the traditional curtains on the inside. I love everything about it – the lights and the Cadillac emblem, and even the rollers and stoppers so the casket will slide in smoothly and not move around when it is in there.

Once, I hopped in and lay down to see what the ceiling looked like. Not that anyone who would be in that position would be able to see the ceiling, but I wanted to know that everything about it was perfect.

I have been known to hop in a casket to see what it's like. I can only do it with the lid off. I couldn't get in if someone put the lid on, because I'm a bit claustrophobic. I would completely freak out. On planes, I have to sit in an aisle seat. In cars, I have to sit in the front. And before I get in a lift, I'll look in to see how full it is. If it's not too full, I stand by the door and face the people, not the door or the walls. And if it stops and a lot of people are obviously going to get in, then I will get out and take the stairs.

One area that has got very creative in recent years is caskets. I love that more and more people are interested in getting something that's not the traditional pine – or mahogany – box. A lot of people want to make their own and I think that's great too. Of course, we have to check them first to make sure the body won't fall out or the handles won't come off so the casket comes crashing down when the pallbearers are halfway out of the church.

So many things in the world today are polished and plastic-looking; it's great to see something that looks a bit rough and handmade. Sometimes people have made caskets out of wood from around their home or property – I think that's some beautiful symbolism there. It's appropriate because the casket is that person's final shelter.

There was a time when funeral directors discouraged this – I think because it represented a loss of profit. I looked at that when the trend started and realised we do miss out on that revenue, but that's just how it needs to be. And the demand is so great now that you just have to go along with it. Decorating caskets is a big thing, sometime with panels that children – and adults – can draw or write messages on.

Some companies specialise in caskets with a difference. One of the advantages of arranging funerals well in advance of someone dying is that you have time to organise extra touches. Dying Art makes them with flashing lights and air-brushed murals. Western Caskets also make caskets to order. If you have a Resene paint chart, you can just give the casket company the code of the colour you want and they will match it. For instance, you could buy a standard purple casket that they keep in stock, or you could choose a darker or lighter shade of purple off the chart. Purple is very popular now. And they can turn it around in a couple of days. But it's a bit hard to do a mural on a casket with three days to go before a funeral.

I have a beautiful casket in stock that has Leonardo Da Vinci's *Last Supper* carved in relief on the sides. We also bring in the domed American caskets, which have some amazing features like a little 'message in the bottle' type phial with a rubber seal that goes into a tiny hole in the corner of the coffin. People can write a special blessing or message on a piece of paper and it will be put in the phial and inserted into a corner of the casket and remain with the loved one forever. Others have a special key that you turn to lock them – when you do, you can actually hear the air being sucked out of the casket.

We have a model where you can adjust the base up and down or left and right to give you a better view of the body. We can also put special photos into the lid of the casket – perhaps a holy picture or a portrait of the loved one's family.

Some families want to go to great lengths to make sure the casket is symbolic of the person inside it. They might want it to be the person's favourite colour, or have a more natural look, if he was a builder, for instance.

Sometimes people have made caskets out of wood from around their home or property – I think that's some beautiful symbolism there. It's appropriate because the casket is that person's final shelter.

Pacific Island families like something stately and impressive, such as the big domed American style caskets.

I think it's good for people to think about the right casket for an individual. I get a little sad if someone is in something I know they wouldn't have liked.

But the single most important thing about a casket is that it is the right size for the person who's going in it. And some of those persons can be very big. It's not unusual for me to have a couple of people in one day who are more than 180 kilos. Thank goodness we have a hoist to move them from place to place, or I would have to employ a staff of bodybuilders.

As the average size of the population in general has got bigger, the standard width and depth of a casket has had to increase. It used to be 21 inches by 12; now it is 22 inches by 13.

YOU LEARN A LOT about people when they are dead.

The body is in our care and brought back to the funeral home. It's naked, we wash it down, and dry it. It is laid out on the dressing table with a towel and sheet over it. And at that point everyone is the same. Without a person's clothes or make-up or familiar hair style, there is not much to distinguish anyone from anyone else.

At that point, the family arrive and put the clothes on and do the hair. Or a staff member does it. Then you start to see more of the person's character coming into view. We become what we choose to wear.

If I have just laid the person out and not been part of the dressing process, I am often struck by how different they are when I see them again fully dressed in their own clothes. It's amazing how good they look.

Younger people can be more difficult to dress because often you are given clothes that are a tight fit. Older men with their suits or loose jeans are much easier to dress.

Babies and infants are a different case again. To me, an old person who's lived their life is just a shell. Their wairua may be nearby but the physical object is just that. It's different with a child who has only been on this earth for a short time. They have only just arrived, and then they are gone. You can't help wanting to treat them more tenderly, as if they are still here. When I uplift a baby from the coroner's office, I use a baby car seat.

'I've never seen that before,' said a staff member one day when I arrived at the coroner's with my car seat. She was a woman who had worked there many years and I thought would have seen just about everything. The baby I was collecting was only two months old.

'What do other funeral directors do?' I asked, being nosy.

'Some put them on a stretcher with a belt. Some have a sort of carry-cot.'

The car seat just seemed natural to me. The family were waiting for me to come out with this baby and I could tell seeing baby in the car seat made it feel more natural to them. It was as though baby hadn't quite gone yet.

Kaiora and I have had so many babies of our own in the time we have been funeral directors that any time we deal with a baby's death it is close to home. Once when Kaiora was going to collect a little girl, I suggested she let me do it. Having always wanted a girl and never had one of our own, it's even harder to take it in our stride. This was an especially beautiful little girl, and I know Kaiora would have broken down at the sight.

So instead she put her effort into decorating the little girl's casket. Babies' caskets are beautiful because you can put so much personality into them. I think they could be made even more creative and less formal. At the moment, they are like miniature adult caskets, but I don't see why they couldn't be all sorts of different shapes and materials with stickers and other decorations to give them personality.

With babies, even more than in other cases, whānau like to be involved in all aspects of preparation. Again – this is a difference between babies and adults. Adults look after themselves when they are alive, and it's not part of their family's role to dress them and put them to bed and so on. But with babies, that is exactly what we do because they can't do those things yet.

If baby has died, Mum or Dad might like to make a little casket and the family will sew and decorate a mattress and trimmings. Then the older brothers and sisters can paint the outside. Everyone will do whatever they can to make that little baby comfortable because this will be their only chance. We do provide baby caskets, but we don't show them in our display room because some things are just too sad for people to see.

Embalming a child is a lot more difficult than embalming an adult. Everything is so tiny. You need to inject the chemical into very small vessels. We don't use much and it is a very delicate job. You have to keep your eye on the baby the whole time because it can quickly change colour or the face can become bloated and puffed up. Even the suturing up is a very fine process. Because of the effort that is involved we have to charge, but I'd like to see a time when any funeral work for someone under five years old is free.

We don't charge for stillborn babies, though. They are a different case again. There are a few hundred of these every year in New Zealand. Often people don't want a funeral for a stillbirth. It's different from a baby who is a little older, because the parents have never known this child outside the womb. They might keep the baby at home for a little while first, but often they will go straight to the cemetery.

Another complication is that if a baby has been stillborn, it is often because the mother has had a serious medical problem too, and she may have to stay in hospital for quite a while. We can hold Baby until the mother is released. We will have a karakia and then they will take Baby to the cemetery.

WE HAVE GOOD PROCESSES for dealing with everybody that comes into our care.

'We know you'll look after our mum,' the families tell me.

Of course, I could embalm Mum in a couple of hours and have her in the dressing room for the night and everything would be okay. We will do the hair and make-up properly and present her beautifully.

But I think 'look after' means a lot of things. It means spending time with Mum and respecting her and treating her well at every stage of the process.

Sometimes when we are moving Mum's limbs, they don't move so easily. 'Looking after' then doesn't mean being very gentle. It means shaking the rigor mortis out of her arm so that it will be supple enough to get it through the sleeve of her dress.

We have to use needles going up over the nose and under the jawline to sew the mouth closed. It's quite tough, but it is

To me, an old person who's lived their life is just a shell. Their wairua may be nearby but the physical object is just that. It's different with a child who has only been on this earth for a short time.

no different from the sort of things that happen to living people undergoing surgery. They look brutal, but they have to be done to get the best result – to 'look after' the person.

If the family saw it, they would say, 'Don't do that,' so although I like families to be involved as much as possible, it is better that they don't see some of what we have to do.

But I will tell Mum every step of the way that what is happening to her is being done to make her look beautiful.

And she will.

'I au e tuawhitu, i au e turama, i a te māiaia'

A traditional farewell used by the people of Ngāpuhi/Hokianga
to send the spirits of loved ones on their way

CHAPTER EIGHT

POST-MORTEMS AND PAPERWORK

POST-MORTEMS, EMBALMING, CREMATION and death certificates – there are a lot of processes surrounding death that are part of the funeral director's daily routine. People might know their names but not know what they actually involve. I think it is good for people to understand as much as possible of what we do because some of them will be things that will happen to them one day.

QUALIFIED SUCCESS

By 2016, I had worked at two fine funeral companies, started my own reasonably successful business, and had absolutely no professional training. I knew how to do funerals and I knew what the legal requirements about the process were. Colleagues had passed on their knowledge to me as I went along and we were kept up to date every time something changed in, for instance, the *Coroners Act*. But I only got my qualification in 2016, and Kaiora got hers in 2017.

The public assume we need professional qualifications in order to practise, but we don't. Not only are people surprised to learn their funeral director may not be qualified, they're also surprised to hear what the training involves. It's a one-year course, and the bum-on-a-seat part is only six weeks. You do the rest of your course at work.

I loved every single minute of my training, when I finally did it. Not coming from a funeral directing background, it was the first time I got to focus fully on learning about the business and to mix with other funeral directors who didn't have the same bosses as I did, so had different ways of doing things. I felt totally in my world.

The course was held at WelTec in Wellington. Our tutor, Pierre Erasmus, was originally from South Africa and had worked all over the world. As well as knowing a lot about mainstream European funerals, he knew so much about Māori funerals and culture you would think he was a Māori himself.

There were fourteen of us and I happened to be not only one of the youngest, but also the longest-serving funeral director. When Kaiora did the course a year later, there were more than twice as many students, and I have since heard the course has reached its maximum of thirty-two.

I really enjoyed learning about the history of Pākehā funerals in New Zealand. I heard how Pākehā people were originally hands-on when caring for their dead – the opposite of how they are today. They did everything themselves in the home. Then, gradually, they started employing the local cabinetmaker to make the coffins. Then that person took on the job of driving the body to the next stop. Then some cabinetmakers built chapels on their own premises so everything could be done there. I thought that was a beautiful process.

And I was intrigued that Pākehā had turned 180 degrees and taken a hands-off approach for so long. Now they trust the funeral director to do everything, whereas Māori want the funeral director's involvement to be as little as possible.

Because I had been working so long as a funeral director, I already knew a lot of the official curriculum. Where I really benefited was in what I learnt from sharing with my fellow students.

'We do it this way.'

'Really?'

'Well, we do it that way.'

'Wow.'

All of the legalities around funerals and funeral directing are taught at the course and tested rigorously. This includes things like what you can and cannot do and still call it a funeral. New Zealand is blessed because there is not a lot that is compulsory. And there is a lot of flexibility over what a funeral can involve, as long as it is in good taste and not offensive to the public – although that is very debatable and subjective.

For instance, a family might want to have the funeral under a favourite tree at a park up the road. That might be the place where Dad liked to sit and watch the world go by, so it is especially significant. There is no reason for that not to happen if we go through the proper consent process. That's not much more than ringing the council, promising to keep the lid on and making sure the public aren't disturbed.

What is offensive can be debatable and even depend on who is there to see it.

You can have a funeral on a beach, but that is one time when you shouldn't stay between the flags, even if Dad was a lifetime member of the surf lifesaving club. It's best to go off somewhere a bit more discreet.

We can arrange burials at sea – there are guidelines for that. Home cremations are not on, although people have suggested it on large properties. People are realistic. They might want to bury Mum on the farm, but they know that can't happen. Most are happy with the alternative of having a cremation at the crematorium and then scattering the ashes at the farm.

At the moment, there are a lot of families applying to councils to set up their own cemeteries. This is especially so for Māori families, wanting to create an identity for themselves with a tūrangawaewae. Obviously we have to be mindful of other demands on land and how scarce it is going to become.

Cremation is the space-saving option and the tidiest way to go. But according to tikanga, disposal of a body is about allocating places for the bones to be placed eventually.

Getting permission to have your own urupā is a lengthy process but we are going through it ourselves in my family at the moment. Kaiora and her family are building their own cemetery at Pawarenga. It's up a hill, so there are some logistical challenges, but we will get there. She is connected because of the land her father gave to the family.

DOCTORS IN THE HOUSE

The paper trail is not as long as it used to be, thanks to computerisation in areas such as getting a death certificate. This is a legal requirement for every funeral. Just as everyone has to have a birth certificate when they are born, they also have to have a death certificate at the other end of life. You get signed in, and you get signed out.

Its official name is Medical Certificate of Cause of Death, and you have to have one if the deceased is more than twenty-eight days old when they die. It means a doctor has confirmed the cause of death.

The certificate serves a few purposes. It enables data to be collected on what people in New Zealand are dying of. It also (hopefully) ensures there has been no foul play in the case of a sudden death.

The doctor signing the certificate has to have seen the person within the three months before their death. If it was three months and one day, then the coroner takes charge. It's frustrating but I feel it is better to be safe than sorry.

If the body is to be buried and the regular GP is not available, a doctor from the same practice is able to sign the death certificate if he or she is able to see the GP's notes.

And if the body is going to be cremated, a doctor can view the body and issue the certificate even if they have never seen that person alive. Often we will uplift a body, put it in the car and drive to a clinic to show it to the doctor there. Then we can get on with our job.

Nowadays, a doctor can sign the certificate online by going to deathdocs.services.govt.nz. But as recently as 2014, we could have a lot of trouble organising these.

For instance, say someone was seeing a doctor at a medical centre that was open from Monday to Friday, from nine to five. If the person died at five-thirty on Friday afternoon, when all the doctors had gone home, it was quite possible you wouldn't be able to find a doctor to help until Monday morning, which meant the body had to stay at the funeral home or the coroner's office over the weekend.

Legally, we are not allowed to do much until we have a death certificate or the coroner has said we can take the person. That proves difficult for many families.

To this day it saddens me, because I know that a lot of people will carry that stress through their lives. I know because people who have been through it tell me about it and how it has cast a shadow over the whole process for them.

Back then if we couldn't find a doctor, people would say, 'My mother is going to go off if Francis doesn't take her.' But the alternative was for the coroner to take over and keep the body in the fridge for the weekend.

It was a very difficult situation. Some practices had after-hours doctors on call, but they didn't necessarily know the patient.

Now, thanks to deathdocs, in most cases a GP can do everything on their phone.

POST-MORTEMS

If someone dies unexpectedly from an unknown cause, the body is referred to the coroner and taken into their jurisdiction. The coroner's job is to collect all the necessary information that will determine the cause of death. The coroner doesn't touch or sometimes even see the body. He or she is a lawyer who reads through notes to make sure it's evidence-based and everything is done by the law.

Most of the time, when a body is taken into the care of the coroner, a post-mortem takes place. The body cavity and the head are opened up, and the organs are taken out to be dissected and sent to the lab for blood tests, a toxicology report and so on.

If someone who has appeared to be healthy drops dead at the gym (which happens quite a lot; be careful how much running you do) it can be determined whether too much exercise was the cause. In general, people are more likely to die from too little exercise rather than too much, but that's another story. Anyway, the coroner – and the person's family – want to know why this heathy specimen dropped dead.

After the pathologist and mortuary assistants have examined all the organs and done all the tests, they put the bits into a nice clear bag, pop it back inside and sew the tummy up.

At that point, the funeral home, who may have been contacted at the start of the process, will liaise with the coroner's office to organise the uplifting of the body. We take it back to our mortuary to prepare for embalming.

Difficulties arise when families have to wait for a post-mortem. This can lead to a great deal of anguish. Māori families are used to a turnaround time of three to four hours between a death and taking a body into their care. That's not usually a problem. If I uplift someone in the morning, by twelve o'clock that body can be dressed and in the casket ready to go on the marae.

But in the case of a post-mortem, the coroner has the final say – and how long the whānau must wait depends on him or her. Naturally, the coroner wants to do their job properly and make sure the correct cause of death has been determined. It may not just be a case of deciding whether or not foul play has been involved. The person may have had an undiagnosed, hereditary medical condition that might have serious implications for the rest of the family.

You can have a wait of several days depending on the coroner's workload and the circumstances of the death. Car accidents and suicides can add to the complications. For me as a funeral director, trying to balance the legal process with tikanga and tangihanga is a juggling act.

I understand the coroner's process and the reasons for it. If that was my loved one, I'd want them to do whatever was necessary to find the cause of death.

But family members don't always appreciate this, especially when they are dealing with shock and are in the depths of grief. I can get hammered over that: 'Francis, what is going on? ... I thought you'd get the body ... Why is it taking so long?' After all, we are called Tipene Funerals – we present ourselves as Māori funeral directors, sensitive to tikanga and Māori expectations, so it's bad if we can't meet those expectations.

Sometimes, it's not until after the tangi that the family will recognise the need to know the cause of death and be grateful for it. But they're still not happy about the delay.

Cases of children or infants are the worst. Whenever I get a baby that will be referred to the coroner, I am so stressed. The family object to a post-mortem and I understand that totally. The thought of a baby being put through that is horrible and it stirs up powerful emotions.

But my more rational side tells me the wairua has gone. All that is left is a shell. That's why we call dead people tūpāpaku, meaning 'hollow vessel'.

But you can't explain that to someone in grief, and you shouldn't try.

You can have a funeral on a beach, but that is one time when you shouldn't stay between the flags, even if Dad was a lifetime member of the surf lifesaving club. It's best to go off somewhere a bit more discreet.

THE ANCIENT ART

For many people, the shell that is left after death is the person they loved. That is all that remains of them, so they want to preserve it by embalming. It's a way of holding on a little longer to what has been lost. That's the emotional reason for it.

It's been practised for thousands of years. In ancient Egypt the internal organs were removed, and incense and other substances put in their place to dry and preserve the body. In modern embalming, combinations of chemicals including formaldehyde and methanol are injected into the blood system to get the same result.

Practically, it serves three purposes: sanitation, preservation and presentation.

I know how to do embalming but we don't have a mortuary with all the necessary equipment for it in our homes, so we use the services of a wonderful freelancer called Rikki Solomon and his whānau. (Yes – even embalming can be a family business, just like funeral directing.)

He does an amazing job. More than that – he is a saviour, helping us do the best for our families while staying in the background himself. His job is to perform small miracles every day by making people look the way their loved ones want to remember them. He has been doing it brilliantly for about twenty-five years.

While he and I both deal with dead people, my job is mainly about helping the living, whereas Rikki spends all day every day with dead bodies. This may explain something I have noticed about embalmers over the years – when they are outside the mortuary, in social situations, they are very, very talkative. It must be nice actually being able to hold a conversation with someone who will talk back to you. They love getting out and meeting people.

Embalming is not something I could do as a full-time job, even though I learnt the basics of how to do it from Ramsey Joyce Jr when I was at Lagoon View. He was thorough, clever and very patient – which anyone who tries to teach me anything has to be.

He had an amazing grasp of the embalming processes and the science behind it. I still understand only a fraction of that. He taught me formulas and how to mix chemicals according to the cause of death, the size, the skin colour, even how long the tangi will be – all those things get taken into account.

Not only was he good at the science of embalming, he was also a fantastic make-up artist who made the people he worked on look incredible. We have a lot of make-up in the funeral homes.

Unfortunately, make-up is not really a big deal with Māori and Pacific Island funerals because we touch and kiss so much. You can do a great make-up job on someone and then along comes Aunty and she takes hold of the face and covers it in kisses – and all the make-up comes off.

We still use make-up on Māori and Pasifika people, especially if there has been some sort of physical trauma, but then we ask mourners to be extra careful. That's one case where the fact that Pākehā are a bit more reserved when it comes to physical demonstrations of emotion works in our favour.

People want to see their relatives as they knew them. In the case of Pasifika people, if a person has been suffering a long time and that has radically changed their appearance, the family may not want to see them after death. They want to remember them as they were, so they will query whether embalming is necessary.

Not because of the expense – they hardly ever worry about cost – but possibly because they have had a bad experience with embalming in the past. The result of a bad embalming job can be more upsetting than none at all.

A lot of time goes into making someone look as natural as we can. Don't give them a frown. Don't pull the mouth too far back. Don't close the eyes or mouth too tight, so they look especially grim, or not enough so they look as though they are trying to talk. Those are some of my pet hates.

One of the hardest parts of embalming is getting the eyes and mouth right. We call it feature setting and it is so difficult because usually you are operating from a photograph. And nine times out of ten, the photo you get will be of the person with their eyes open and smiling. When you see someone resting in their casket, you do not want them to have their eyes open and be smiling. You expect them to have their eyes and mouth shut, which usually only happens when we are asleep. When you think about it, we don't get seen in our sleep by many people, so it is hard for the embalmer to know what a person should look like. Maybe as part of their funeral planning, people should get a nice photo taken with their mouth and eyes shut.

There are two types of modern embalming: post-mortem embalming and standard embalming.

Post-mortem embalming is the kind I have explained, where the organs are removed and put back again. It is more work-intensive, but it is a nice way to embalm because once the body has been opened up you can see everything. You can inject your chemicals in exactly the right place because the arteries are open and visible. We wash and clean the inside, make sure all the organs are there and introduce some chemicals to the viscera bag. Then we inject chemicals into the rest of the body to make a lifelike presentation.

Standard embalming is quite simple. Two incisions are made in the right and left carotid arteries below the neck and a chemical introduced to give a lifelike appearance, and to preserve and sanitise the body.

Compared to post-mortem embalming, however, it is like trying to fix a vehicle without looking under the bonnet. You have to keep checking and testing as you go along.

These days, with many diseases and the many medicines that have been introduced into our bodies to make us live longer, it's getting harder and harder for the embalming chemicals to do their job. They have to work against all these medicines in the body.

Where people have been in hospital a long time and been on all sorts of medication, especially if they have been on life support, embalming is also much more difficult.

The death certificate can make our job easier because the more we know about the person's medical history, the easier it is to work out what we may need to do to preserve them. For example, if there has been a blood thinner used, that is good for us. It means we will have a good flow to get the blood draining.

I'm so grateful to have a total pro like Rikki on hand to take all these factors into account and ultimately help the people who trust us with the care of their loved ones.

A lot of people question the need to embalm and many decide not to. I love that too.

DUST TO DUST

When it comes to choosing a way to dispose of the dead, cremation is the simplest option, but in our business, burial is still the alternative most people choose.

There are arguments for and against both processes.

There are good green arguments against putting more people in the ground. The land we live on has to be protected and preserved. Open space is becoming scarcer, and filling it up with dead bodies may not be the best use of it.

On the other hand, burial is a beautiful ritual and allows you to erect a wonderful headstone to pay tribute to the person there. The symbolism of returning someone to the earth from which they came is powerful.

People often ask how long a body will last in a grave. And the correct answer is: I don't really know. The length of time can vary a lot because so many factors can affect it. It all depends on things like how wet the terrain is, whether it is on a slope, how close it is to any tidal movements. Ultimately everything will be absorbed into the earth, but there is no knowing exactly when.

I did a disinterment at Waikumete for a man who had been in the ground at the top of a hill for sixty years. If he had been at the bottom where all the water should run to, you might have expected him to be in bad shape. But there at the top of the hill, his body had completely gone. There were just a couple of teeth and his fully intact, solid wood casket. That blew my mind.

In general, it is the caskets that don't last very long. After five years, all that might be left are the plastic handles and silver screws.

I would love to do some research on this and study how long different caskets last and how long bodies survive in different environments. I have thought about getting some sheep and doing an experiment. Obviously if you just put an empty casket in the ground you wouldn't get a very scientific result. But sheep would behave roughly like a human body and you could test them in all sort of conditions – up high, down low, in wet areas and dry areas, and so on.

Even though there is not much left after a cremation, those remains in an urn on the mantelpiece may be more secure for longer than a body that has been buried. You are safe in the ground only until someone decides they want to build a motorway through a cemetery – as happened with Auckland's Grafton Cemetery, from which more than four thousand bodies were dug up and buried elsewhere in the 1960s.

Or your plot of cemetery land might be taken over to build state houses. At Mangere Lawn Cemetery, the only thing that separates the people at rest from the state housing next door is a simple fence. I sometimes wonder if the people who live in those houses wake up in the morning, have their Milo and wish good morning to all the dead people at their door.

There is no denying that burial is a lot more expensive than cremation. In New Zealand in 2019, purchasing a gravesite cost between $5000 and $8000; a cremation was around $600.

But most people don't make their decisions based on price, even when I point out to them how they can avoid spending money.

In Māori and Pacific Island culture, burials are by far the most popular choice, although we are starting to see some changes there. Not long ago, I was doing 90 per cent burials and 10 per cent cremations; now about 25 per cent of all our funerals end at the crematorium. I'm sure that number will continue to grow.

Attending a cremation is an eye-opener for many Māori and Pacific Island families who have never experienced what it is about.

When I took my grandmother to the cremation of one of our whānau not long ago, it was the first time she had ever attended one. She was in the chapel and saw the TV screens come down, the photo presentation and people speaking, and at the end she heard music playing and saw the casket lowered to be taken away. She didn't see the fire light up.

'That was so beautiful,' she said at the end.

'No, you're not going to be cremated,' I said.

The actual cremation process is very simple and efficient: a casket goes into a giant oven which incinerates (nearly) all the contents. That's all there is to it. The length of time it takes depends on the size of the body. For a small, thin person, it will all be over in around two hours. Bigger people take a bit longer.

Then there is a cooling-down period, after which the metal bits, such as casket screws, are taken out. What is left is scraped together and goes into a cremulator. The flesh and the wood have all gone up in smoke, but even after being exposed to the fierce high temperatures of the cremator, there will usually be some bone left. The cremulator spins around with metal balls that smash the remaining bone into fine ash.

The same questions come up time and time again over cremation. Some of them have been around nearly a hundred years.

For example: 'Do we take the handles off the casket before it is cremated?'

No.

This usually goes back to a concern about money – why should people pay for something that is going to be incinerated? Many people can only just afford to keep themselves alive, let alone pay extra when someone is dead.

In fact, with cremations they don't even have to pay for a casket to be destroyed in the process. We have a cremation casket they can have, which doesn't come with handles. A simple casket is put inside a more elaborate, presentation style one for the funeral. When we get to the crematorium, the body is taken out of that and just the liner and body are cremated. People can make that choice.

For others, that would never do. Some families buy beautiful caskets with elaborate Māori carving on them for thousands of dollars and are happy for it all to go up in smoke. That's their choice.

But in all cases, we do not recycle handles or anything else that has been paid for. It wouldn't be legal or ethical; it wouldn't even be possible, because the crematoria have a lot of staff and there are security cameras everywhere.

The only time we might take handles off a casket at a cremation is if the handles make the whole thing too wide to get through the furnace door. If that's the case, we remove the handles and put them into the cremator on top of the casket.

Second question: 'Does my mum or dad get cremated with other bodies?'

No.

In New Zealand, only one body can fit into the cremator at a time. Two people could not be put in together to save money, even if anyone wanted to do something that was so disrespectful.

There is one exception, and that is if a child and parent are being farewelled together, perhaps because they have both been killed in a car accident. Then people often want a double cremation and, as sad as it sounds, that is a beautiful thing.

Sometimes it's not enough for people to see the coffin go off somewhere vague. Another part of the cremation that many people like is called 'viewing the charge'. They sit in front of a window that is covered with a beautiful curtain. The curtain opens, revealing the door of the cremator. Then that opens and the family watches the casket go into the cremator. The door is closed, then the curtain, and that is the end of the ceremony. It is like seeing the body go into the ground at a burial.

This way they can see a bit more of the process and that can provide peace of mind. It all depends on the individual. Some people can't handle it. Some people insist on it.

OUR PLACE

People are always curious about what is 'behind the scenes' at a funeral home. Well, thanks to *The Casketeers*, not many parts of our building are behind the scenes. But there are a few places that I can describe for you now, if you'd like to come on a virtual tour.

Before we moved into our current building, it had been the premises of an old Auckland funeral directing firm, J Weir & Co. It is a big two-storey building in a semi-industrial part of town. The previous occupants used only the street half of the ground floor for their day-to-day business. The rest was storage and a garage.

When we took over, we converted the top storey into an apartment for our family. It was spacious with enough room for all our kids, and it was convenient being so close to the business. If something came up at short notice, it took us as long to get there as it did to walk downstairs.

But it was also inconvenient being so close to the business as it meant we were never able to get away, which is why we were happy to move the family out when Tipene Funerals outgrew the downstairs space. That said, the growing hasn't stopped and now we have really outgrown this whole building, so we have taken over another nearby to store cars and caskets.

The space that used to be our bedroom is now our office and I sometimes think it is the worst thing that has ever happened to this business. Kaiora and I share it with a cot and a play seat for Francis Jr, who is often in here with us. Every inch of the floor and walls is covered with all sorts of things – from kids' toys and drawings to pictures of Jesus to photos of our tūpuna. There is a giant CCTV screen on one wall so we can keep an eye on what is happening in any part of the building at any time. There is a fridge that I definitely shouldn't have in here because it is not good for my diet. My desk has a big computer I don't really need because I only use it for browsing on Trade Me and wasting my time (and money, when I find things I like). And just outside there is a toilet and small kitchen. So really we could survive in the office for a long time if we had to.

But the worst of it is that it has separated us from the other staff. It is like our own little den – Francis and Kaiora's space – that people are reluctant to enter. And we have installed ourselves at the top of the building, as though we are above everything else that goes on here. Other funeral directors have offices on this level, but they aren't fortresses like ours.

You can do a great
make-up job on someone
and then along comes
Aunty and she takes hold
of the face and covers
it in kisses – and all the
make-up comes off.

We are so busy and everyone has so many needs and demands we have had to sacrifice the closeness we had with our staff just to keep everything going. There are a whole lot of contradictions now. Being up here feels like we are running away from the work, but the work we do here is important as well. And we have cut ourselves off with phones. When we were all downstairs, people used to poke their head around the door if they wanted to talk to us. Or we were just hanging around and accessible. Now they ring from downstairs and say, 'Francis, are you available to speak to so and so?'

The phone system is another nuisance. People can always get a human on one of our cellphone numbers. But if they ring the office number, they hear 'For reception, press one, etc.,' because the business now has so many parts to it that we have had to introduce one of those systems.

The office next to ours has four funeral directors squeezed into it with their work stations. They organise everything from here – bookings, meetings, viewings, catering. And we also store the hair dryers and the big make-up kits in here. We are just like any other make-up artists – we have to have every possible kind of make-up for every possible kind of colouring and complexion, which means we need to keep a lot on hand. And of course, there is a vacuum cleaner. We have a lot of vacuum cleaners at Tipene Funerals. Thanks to the bargains on Trade Me, I've been able to source things that all look super shiny and new for the staff to use.

We also have a reception area upstairs, for when all the downstairs spaces are full. There is a display cabinet showing various kinds of urns that can be used to store ashes. They come in all sizes. I love the single rosebud one that holds just a small portion of ashes. That's a lovely idea if everyone wants to have a memento of a loved one. It would look great placed on a wall in someone's home. And there are scattering urns too – you can take the lid off and scatter the ashes in the sea or wherever without them blowing back in your face.

But most of what goes on goes on downstairs. For instance, the first thing people see when they come through the front door is the reception desk. It really is the face of Tipene Funerals. It's in a small foyer space with a few seats where people can wait to be looked after. To the right are the stairs that lead to the upstairs offices. To the left are the other parts of the business. And immediately behind reception, in a space that might be good for keeping some brooms and mops, is my funeral director Fiona's office that she refuses to move out of even though she has well and truly outgrown it. It's a bit like Doctor Who's TARDIS would be if the TARDIS actually wasn't any bigger inside than it looks from the outside. I've tried to get her to move into a bigger one or let me make this one bigger, but she just says no and I don't have the strength for that fight.

The biggest space downstairs is our chapel, which can hold up to 160 people. We can divide it in two for smaller funerals. Nothing looks worse than a funeral with just a few people spread out in a big room.

In our dressing rooms, we keep everything that might be needed to clothe the body. We have a sort of bed that we use to make it more homely, which is lovely when the family decide they want to take part in the process.

I keep a lot of spares here: there is hairspray, artificial roses and most importantly spare underwear, stockings, scarves and socks in all sizes and colours. I learnt about that the hard way because there were so many occasions when we would find we didn't have something and a family member would say, 'I'll just pop home and get some,' and ninety minutes later you would still be waiting and not able to do anything else until they got back. This is one of the few things we do here that isn't about the customer's convenience – it's about mine.

A hospital donated a table for us to dress the bodies on. It is adjustable up and down, which means most staff are able to alter it so they can slide the bodies on and off to get them in and out of the caskets. It wasn't quite wide enough for today's larger bodies when I got it, so I cut a thick plywood base and now it works perfectly.

Just along from this room is the casket display area. I always keep it brightly lit, partly so it's not scary, but also because it makes them all look so beautiful. I make sure there is a wide variety available as anyone who comes in here can see. We have a lot of caskets with wow appeal – like the ones with murals on or the elaborately carved Māori ones.

When it comes to fitting out the caskets, we also have lot of options for people to choose from. Side sets – the fabric pieces that line the caskets – come in all sorts of designs. For instance, we have a beautiful Māori tukutuku pattern. That's very popular. We have a denim version that young people like, and there is a bright yellow one that is very popular with members of the Killer Beez gang, because that is their colour. People of the Ratana faith like purple.

It's all about presentation and what the families see, because funerals are for the living. Of course, we have our plain, simple and very economical caskets on display too. And most people just want plain rimu or mahogany.

Behind the casket display area is our miniature music studio. It has all the electronic controls for the lights and music during services. The computer runs the slide shows.

A more recent addition to the facilities that I really love is some extractor fans for the inside toilets. I had problems with the smell of poos inside so I spent $4000 on new units. They work perfectly and you can barely hear them. Now there's never any smell.

THERE ARE SOME INVISIBLE traditions here, things you wouldn't know just from looking at the building and what's inside. Basically, we follow tikanga for how we handle dead bodies and keep as closely as possible to the sort of things you would do on a marae.

For instance, we have a certain door we bring the bodies in through. There are other doors we never take them through, such as the front door. The body has to go out through the door it came in. However, it is okay for babies to go through the front door because they are considered pure in God's eyes. The rest of us are all sinners. Those are Māori traditions acknowledging the difference between the living and the dead.

We keep water outside the dressing room and chapel for sprinkling and symbolic cleansing, just as you would find at an urupā or a marae.

We usually have a karakia at the end of a visit with a family. After we have arranged the funeral or had a meeting with them, we just take a few moments for a short prayer. But only if they are open to that – we always ask first.

We don't eat or drink around bodies, as that is Māori tradition. But that's not necessarily how other people do things. We're not inflexible. I don't think Pākehā people should have to keep to Māori traditions. They don't believe in what we believe in – and they are the ones paying us. And the same goes for Pacific Island people. They just have different traditions from ours. So if the Pākehā want to take their coffee into the viewing room when they go to visit Mum, that is fine. And Pasifika people have a custom of eating around the deceased, so it's important they can keep to that tradition.

But not our staff. If we are doing a walk-through in the morning and they have their coffees with them, they leave them outside when we go into a room where a body is. We don't need to tell them that – they already know.

A COUPLE OF FUNERAL DIRECTORS

Kaiora: I do funerals sometimes. I have done the training and am fully qualified. There's nothing really I can't do, although if I've just had a baby, the staff don't like me lifting things and doing other work. Most of my activity is behind the scenes, but when there is time or we are super busy, I am happy to conduct funerals myself. There always seems to be a lot of juggling to do with everything that is going on between family and home and work.

Sometimes I share duties with Francis. For instance, the usual procedure for Māori funerals is to start with a karakia, do a basic mihi and then the whānau will go on their way. Francis does the mihi and I will follow that up with a waiata. That's my duty. It's what I do.

It enhances the kōrero.

It's funny that the teaching in Māoritanga that my father instilled in me in my early years is coming back to the surface now and being used in this way. I am so grateful for his teaching, even if its purpose wasn't clear at the time.

It's lucky Francis and I like each other so much, when we live together and then come to work and sit in the same office all day – with Francis Jr in the middle between our desks.

I can get frustrated with things, but I miss Francis when he isn't here. I can be really focused on doing something and caught up in my work to the point that I don't notice when he is out and I have no idea where he is.

I'll send a text: 'Where are you?'

'I'm with that family arranging the funeral. I thought I told you.'

'Oh, so you did. Sorry.'

There are certainly some challenges working together. The financial management causes conflict. I would like us to have some, but it can be hard to talk to Francis about money.

He has trouble understanding that we have two very different types of communication. There is wife and husband communication and there is business partner to business partner communication. With the second one, it is not the wife talking. He can't seem to get that out of his head. It is the businessperson who is saying, 'This is your budget. It looks like a lot of money but it is everything we have and we have to use it wisely.' But he can spend impulsively on things we haven't budgeted for.

I just have to do the best I can when that happens. I can't fire him. I can't even give him a first warning. What am I going to do? I juggle. I spend a lot of time borrowing from Peter to pay Paul for Francis.

The good bit about working together is that we are able to bounce off one another about what we have been through in a day and have a debrief. That's healthy and I am so grateful that we can be there for each other then.

We react differently to some of the more extreme cases we confront. Francis has thick skin and he is usually able to put up a shield so things don't get to him. But I sense there are certain cases that hit him hard. When that happens, he tends to shut off and not want to talk to anybody. He just closes the door on the world. I know at some point he will want to talk about whatever it is, but I don't force it out of him. He'll let me know when he's ready and I'll be there.

I FIND SOME SITUATIONS very difficult. The last one where I was emotionally invested was a two-year-old baby. Francis knew he was coming in.

'Are you sure you'll be okay to look after this?' said Francis. 'It's a very sad case.'

'Of course. I want to do it. I know the whaea and she will need support.'

'I'm just not sure your emotions are up to it. Why don't you let me take over?'

'No, no, I can do it.'

But it really hit me.

The grandmother came in. I helped her dress her mokopuna and she was crying the whole time.

'Ka pai, Whaea,' I said gently. 'Come on. You can do that.'

I could only be professional with her. I was holding it in. Our son Moronai was the same age as that baby. But I still had to do my job – dress the baby, get the paperwork done.

I felt so strongly for that poor grandmother – every bit of sadness was right there on the surface and she needed someone to hold her hand through the process. She took a long time and I encouraged her to.

'There is no time limit. Take as long as you like. Take an hour to put Baby's pants on, if you want to.'

After all, these were the last things she would be able to do for her mokopuna and she obviously loved him so much. It was so sad.

It wasn't until she left that I broke down completely. Francis wasn't around and I couldn't wait for him to come home. I saw my kids and just wanted to hug them. You love them so much, and you worry about them so much more if you have just seen a baby who has drowned or been in an accident. You're always on edge with anything they're doing.

Francis came home and saw that I was upset and all I wanted was a hug.

'I told you I wanted to be there with you today,' he said.

'I know,' I said. 'I thought I could manage.'

Also, Francis is only one man. I know he would like to do everything but he can't be everywhere all the time. We have had other cases like that. They are the worst experiences and you wouldn't wish them on anyone.

Haere Otūtutu me te ō, haere Opīwhane me te ō

———————————

Travel the paths to Otūtutu and Opīwhane with sufficient provisions

CHAPTER NINE

WHEN THINGS GO WRONG

THERE IS A GOOD REASON the theory part of a funeral director's training course is so short: it's such a practical job. With any funeral, there are hundreds of things you have to do and get right. And each one of those things could easily go wrong.

On the morning of a funeral, I check the weather first, because that can make a big difference to how things will go. When I have a burial on a day when there is going to be torrential rain and wind, I probably do look like the stereotype of the sad-faced funeral director.

I always call the caterers and others before a funeral – because although it's never happened, one day they might forget altogether. I text the celebrant. I ring the cemetery to make sure the grave has been dug the right size for the casket – or that we have used a casket that is the right size for the grave. I also want to double-check there hasn't been a cave-in overnight, owing to bad weather or something unexpected. I also have to check for all the things that can go wrong between the funeral home or church and the cemetery. What is the traffic like in the morning? Who is riding with us? What is parking like at the venue?

Things do go wrong. It doesn't matter how hard you try to plan and prepare, 'circumstances beyond our control' are always lying there waiting to trip you up. You have to be at peak performance at all times – and sometimes you aren't.

For instance, I learnt a valuable lesson when I went to Middlemore once to collect a body.

'That must be the body there,' said a hospital worker when I arrived to do the removal.

'Thanks,' I said and put the body on the stretcher ready to go. Then I thought to check the ID tag and discovered it was completely the wrong person. I was glad it was me and not one of my staff.

Fortunately, I hadn't got as far as putting the body in the car and taking it away. That would have been awful.

But not as awful as putting a body in the wrong grave, which is one of those fears that give funeral directors nightmares. I've never done it, but I've come too close.

When you go to a public cemetery in Auckland, your funeral is assigned a coloured flag and you follow the flags that are your colour to find your plot. Everyone who's attending the funeral knows they just need to follow the yellow flags and they will end up at the right service. It is a good system, especially when a cemetery might have five funerals in one day and a couple happening at the same time.

It's a lot better than the old system, where you were told your grave was Section B, Row Two, Plot Three. No one knew where

Section B was for a start. And it doesn't help that cemeteries are usually flat – it's that much harder to get oriented.

On this occasion, I had a funeral at Waikumete Cemetery before the days of flags. It was a Mormon family. They don't like being late, so they were almost getting ahead of me, which was making me anxious. This job was one of two burials in the same row that day, and there were no staff around.

In due course, everyone – including me – arrived and we took the casket out of the hearse and began the loved one's last journey. As I walked along with the pallbearers carrying the casket, we came to the freshly dug grave. I was sure that it was our one so I walked a little ahead and started to turn towards the grave. Fortunately, one of the sons spoke up.

'Look, Mum, we've stopped to pay our respects to someone else before we take you to your final resting place.'

I think he was serious. He genuinely thought that was what I was doing. But I was all ready to put her in there and only him speaking up stopped me. So, at the same time I realised my mistake and was saved. I leapt at the opportunity.

'We're just going to bow our heads,' I said softly, 'and then we will go to Mum's resting place because there will be someone else here later.'

Her plot was two spaces over.

That was nearly my unlucky day. I was so fortunate that the family knew where the grave was.

We had a similar experience at the same cemetery another day. Once again, there were two graves in the same row being used on the same day. These were very close together. I wasn't conducting the funeral on that day.

The burial took place normally. They lowered the casket. They backfilled the grave. And then one of the family said, 'Hang on. This is a bit further along than I thought it was. We need to go back.'

I took the call from my funeral director. When he told me, I was beside myself.

'Before you start yelling,' he said, 'it wasn't our fault.'

It wasn't, but you still feel terrible. I always take things like that on.

'What is the family doing? Who is looking after them? And what went wrong?'

We spoke to the cemetery staff and tried very hard not to get caught up in a blame game. We just wanted the body to be put in the right plot and see it settled so the family could be at peace. As it was, it was a very traumatic experience for them.

A week later, we went back, disinterred the body and deposited it in the correct grave.

Those were cases of human error. But the trouble with graves is that most of the things that can go wrong happen underground. We had a case with a huge Tongan funeral that almost came to a standstill at the cemetery because when we got there and looked into the grave we could see an exposed gas pipe.

The cemetery knew they had made the mistake this time. They were very apologetic. But time wasn't on our side with all these mourners who had come from far and wide. It wasn't like they could wait around while things got sorted out. We decided to do the interment then and there and disinter later, so everyone could disperse and we could close off this part of the job.

One of the most interesting burials I've had was at Waikaraka Cemetery, which is right on the Manukau Harbour and a very

The tide was so strong that, even though the sea was about fifty metres away, by the time we got the casket to the bottom of the grave, there was water halfway up the side. It was bouncing on the water like a mad boat.

compact site. There are no new plots there but sometimes those that have been purchased a long time ago have to be opened.

I had to do a burial close to the waterside, so the cemetery staff said we would need to synchronise it with the tide. I had never had to do that before.

When I told the family what time we would need to do the burial, they said the hour didn't suit them. I explained that if we did it when they wanted to, the tide would be so high that there could be some water in the grave. They insisted, so I told them we could go ahead but they would have to be ready for us to use pumps to keep the grave dry during the ceremony, and they were happy with that.

When we got there, there was already water in the bottom of the plot, so we had to have the pump going while the priest was making the final committal. It was a big pump and it seemed to be sending out a tremendous amount of water. There was a hose emptying it metres away but all the noise was very distracting.

The priest was a bit annoyed as this is a particularly solemn time and normally the only sound you hear is his voice saying the beautiful final prayers.

'As soon as you are done,' I said to Father, 'give me the nod and we will turn the pump off, take out the hose and lower the casket.'

He gave me the nod. I gave the sexton the nod. He turned the pump off and we took the hose out of the grave. But the tide was so strong that, even though the sea was about fifty metres away, by the time we got the casket to the bottom of the grave, there was water halfway up the side. It was bouncing on the water like a mad boat. We couldn't put the hose back in, so I signalled to everyone who could to grab a spade and start shovelling. As we tipped the dirt back into the grave it made the most awful noise – splash, splash, splash. The site was turning into a soggy pit.

There was so much water mixed in that we appeared to have a whole grave's worth of soil left over. I've heard of a watery grave, but this was ridiculous.

I brought the hearse over to the site, put on a beautiful Celine Dion CD and turned it up loud enough to drown out the noise. All the people who knew the song sang along and it ended up being a beautiful moment. But it was also one of the strangest burials I've ever done.

The family were very good about it because, fortunately, I had been upfront about what might happen right from the start. Even then, no one expected things to be that bad – least of all me. This was the first time I really understood what a difference the lay of the land, the topography and all the other conditions can make to a burial. I couldn't help thinking about what was happening to all those bodies in all those caskets at the cemetery as the tide went in and out every day.

WHEN I STARTED OUT, I was so worried about things going wrong. I always drove to the cemetery the day before the funeral to check the venue, the route and the parking. I did that for a long time, and with ten to twelve funerals a month it was manageable. Now that we average thirty-five a month it's just not possible, so I cross my fingers and say a karakia instead.

Auckland traffic is like another person is involved in the process and making it more complicated. It can make or ruin a funeral and it is almost impossible to predict what it will be like

When people ask about us storing ashes, I say, 'Yes, we do, but you never know where they might end up.'

on any day, because it's like the weather and can go from pleasant to a nightmare in an instant.

People complain about having to head off to the cemetery early, but there is no choice because there is no knowing how long it might take. It's better to get to the site early and have to wait a few minutes before we can go in than it is to arrive late. Every minute you are late is a minute that comes off the time available to do honour to the deceased at the graveside, which is such an important and beautiful part of the funeral.

If you are having the service at the cemetery chapel and book it for one hour, then you have fifteen minutes grace either side. If it is for noon to one, you have from quarter to twelve till quarter past one. So you had best be hoping and praying that your funeral starts and finishes on time. If it doesn't, you have the next funeral backing up waiting to get in. It's stressful on everyone, including me.

IT'S NOT JUST IN BURIALS that things can go wrong. The most common problem is when people don't collect the ashes. This is universal among funeral directors. I find it quite sad to think that here are people who don't care enough about their relatives to retrieve that small bundle, which is all that is left of them.

I have maybe a dozen sets of unclaimed urns in Onehunga and a few more at the Henderson branch. They nearly all have one thing in common – they are the remains of Pākehā people. Māori and Pacific Island families nearly always get their ashes back as soon as possible.

We do what we can. We contact families and remind them, but you can only do that so many times before making yourself a nuisance.

I have seen firms making public calls for people to collect ashes, and we may have to do that one day. After that there isn't much left we can do, so after a few years I will probably scatter them somewhere beautiful with a simple karakia to make a final farewell.

Two families have asked me to take care of ashes for them in their absence and I was happy to do that. However, it didn't go completely smoothly. I asked the families if I could put them in a garden at the funeral homes and they said that was fine, so I put them in pot plants at the front doors of both homes. As you walk into the funeral homes, you will go past some loved ones. The plants are actually fake, but they have real ashes in them.

Unfortunately, the plants at the door to the Onehunga home got stolen – with the ashes in them. I put a call out on Facebook because I was desperate to get them back. I didn't say they had ashes in them, because it could have got out of all proportion in the media. People were very kind trying to help and it was shared about a thousand times.

We posted a photo from our security camera, and a beautiful member of the public recognised the car and rego plate. We got onto the police and left it to them to investigate from our footage.

Then one day my wife and I were getting our hot chocolates up at Onehunga Mall and we saw the gentleman from our photo. Before I could do anything, Kaiora – complete with a baby in her arms – was off.

'What are you doing?' I said.

'I'm going to get our plants back.'

'Honey, he could be a lunatic, or in a gang.' He was heavily tattooed. That didn't stop her.

'Hey, how does it feel stealing pot plants from a funeral home?'

'What are you on about?' said the man.

'You stole them. You stole pot plants from us and they have ashes of dead people in them.'

He went pale. By that time, I had caught up.

'Darling, calm down,' I said, as I took her back to the car. 'I can look after it.'

Then I went back to the man.

'What can we do to get the pot plants back?' I asked.

'Look, I sold your plants for $160 each,' he said.

'I am so desperate to have them back, sir, can I give you the money to buy them back?'

'Oh no, I sold them, so I will find them one day and I will get them. I'll bring them back. I didn't know they had ashes in them.'

I gave him a card and said, 'Please keep in touch with us.' He was well known to all the shopkeepers up at Onehunga Mall, so I wasn't worried about him disappearing.

Later that day, he rang to say he was still working on it and I knew then we would get them back. We just needed to give him time.

There were two thieves, him and a mate, and a week later they dropped the pot plants off together and apologised. I told the police I didn't want to press charges, but they ended up doing so anyway because the pair had been on a thieving rampage and stolen a lot of stuff.

So when people ask about us storing ashes, I say, 'Yes, we do, but you never know where they might end up.'

Ko Whakatau anahe te toa e ngana ai te tangi a te wahine

———————————

Whakatau alone is the brave, able to appease the cry of the mother

CHAPTER TEN

LOSING LUKE

I HAVE HAD TO TAKE CARE of the funeral arrangements for two people who were close to me. One was my much-loved grandfather, who I will talk about later, who died at the age of seventy-nine.

The other was my cousin Luke Tipene, who was killed in a street fight in Grey Lynn on Halloween night in 2014. He was seventeen years old and the shining light of our extended whānau. My grandfather and his grandmother were brother and sister.

It wasn't just a matter of dealing with the loss of a family member at such a young age; we were all struggling with how he died – after someone lashed out with a broken bottle and he bled to death.

Many funeral directors will go through their whole career without having to deal with anything that close and personal. I wish I hadn't had to.

Luke was a very talented rugby league player with the Glenora Bears club, the kind who is always described as up and coming. In fact, he'd been chosen for some national rep teams.

If you had asked anyone in our family in 2014 to choose a Tipene who was likely to become famous one day, they would have all said Luke. We were sure he was headed for a brilliant international sports career. His whole life had been centred around the club.

His father – my cousin Christopher – died when Luke and his equally sporty twin sister, Kristina, were five years old, and his mum, Terry, had done a great job of raising the twins. What made Luke really special was that, along with league, he was passionate about kapa haka. That combination of his Māori culture and sporting talent made for a formidable package.

Right from his earliest days at school, he had stood out as a natural leader. His peers and younger children always looked up to him and his elders respected him. He took his mana onto the field every time he ran on to play.

He was especially good with little kids. Once, at a family get-together, while all the grown-ups were debating some serious issues, I watched Luke making a special effort with the younger ones, talking to them and kicking a ball around. No one had told him to. Usually teenagers are too busy with each other or their phones to pay the little kids any attention, but Luke wasn't like that.

He gave my son Nikora lots of attention that day. Nikora isn't very sporty and Luke was saying: 'What do you like doing? What do you want to do?' I like all the kids to do something extra-curricular and at that point Nikora was really into dancing. He told Luke how much he loved to dance and Luke took him seriously.

I think Luke's maturity had a lot to do with how much his

death hurt people. I've done funerals of other young people who've been killed in tragedies and they are always sad, but with Luke there was a different feeling because it was so much easier for people to see how much potential had been lost.

EVERY YEAR KAIORA and I put on a Halloween party for the community at our home. We get caskets and props from work to make things spooky and the kids walk through it and try to scare each other. And we have lots of lollies and sausages.

Luke was included in the general invitation in 2014, but how I wish I'd made a point of insisting he come that night.

We were tired and hadn't quite finished putting everything away when we went to bed. I got woken by the phone ringing, which isn't unusual, but it was my Uncle Anton.

'Hey, Francis.'

'Hey, Anton. How are you?'

Naturally when my uncle rings me at that hour I immediately think someone like my aunty must have died.

'It's Lukey.'

'Lukey?'

'Yeah. He's gone.'

Oh, my God. I knew he didn't mean Luke had gone missing down the road. He told me Luke was at Starship, where he'd been taken in the hope he could be saved.

Everyone panicked. Kaiora was so upset. Everyone thought, *Let's get in the car and go up to the hospital*, and that's what we did, with people converging from all different directions.

When I walked in, I could hear my family before I saw them. Being a funeral director was the last thing I felt like. I was in a bit of shock, I'm sure. I didn't ask what happened or for any details. We didn't say a thing. We were there. Everyone just hugged and embraced. No one was able to do anything else, especially think about things like where the body was or what we should be doing about that.

We needed someone to come and break the circuit and fortunately a policeman arrived, followed by the hospital liaison person. These were people I recognised. It was a process I go through every day with different families. Normally, I talk the family through this part but I needed someone else to do it.

The policeman explained the process and by then I was up to asking a few questions. Being a Saturday, it would be usual for them to delay the post-mortem until Monday, especially under the circumstances.

'Is there any possibility that your staff could be around to conduct a post-mortem today so we can get him back to us as a family?' I asked.

Another reason I wanted this was that there was a sense of a lot of anger building up with Luke's mates and people from the different organisations he was involved in. That anger was going to come out somewhere, somehow, and we knew having his physical body would give all those kids a focus for their mourning and somewhere to be rather than roaming around looking for vengeance.

The coronial process isn't very friendly. It's better than it was – when you might have had to wait days to get the body of your loved one back – but it still takes at least twenty-four hours.

It would have been unusual to get his body released any earlier than Monday, but someone spoke to someone and it happened.

I was so grateful. Terry still hadn't seen Luke. He had been taken from the incident to Starship and into theatre and then to the coroner. The police and everyone else worked wonders. And of course, it gave us extra time to be with him as well.

The first time Terry got to see her boy was when I put him in the back of the hearse.

We were in a little side area that was quite private. It wasn't the ideal place, but it was a way for her to see him as soon as possible, given all the formalities that had to be gone through and all the work that would have to be done before the tangi. There is usually a time when we can take the body into a whānau room at the coroner's for us all to have a karakia. But our goal was to get him home quickly because the clock was ticking. Night was falling upon us and there were hundreds of people who needed to see him.

She and the immediate family were there. I opened up the car and lifted the velvet cover on the stretcher. Terry kissed and embraced her dead son. That's not something you ever want to see. Or hear.

You can tell a lot from different cries. There is a sad cry, which is the one you often hear at funerals. But there is also an empty cry, which is what Terry's was. It sounded like there was nothing else she could give out to the universe to show how she was feeling.

I realised how many people would want to see Luke and that it would be hard for Terry and the whānau to have their own time with him. Phones were going constantly as the news spread around the whānau and friends and teammates.

We needed to get him to her whare as soon as possible so the family could be with him. After that karakia at the back of

Everyone got the opportunity to do what they wanted. No one was restricted as to what they could express, and no one had to rush because there was another funeral due.

the hearse, I closed everything up and took him straight to our mortuary to prepare the body.

I find the memory of this night hard to deal with, but at the time I was so focused on doing everything Luke and his family needed that I wasn't thinking about anything like that. I knew how many people were waiting and how desperately his mum and the extended whānau wanted to see him, so the mahi was easy. He was in my physical care so I was responsible for him.

People say to me: 'It must have been so terrible.' No – it's terrible now.

Once we were at the embalmers, it was straight down to work. I hadn't really stopped since that first phone call from my uncle. I stayed for the whole process. Rikki Solomon, the embalmer, and his whānau were there too and they were so considerate and helpful. They guided me through my part in the embalming.

There were some bad lacerations to Luke's face that needed make-up to disguise them. He was a good-looking young guy and he knew it, so I knew he would appreciate anything that made him look better. I even had a giggle about that at the time because I knew what he would be thinking.

Once the preparation and embalming were finished, we put him in the car and shot over to our Henderson funeral home and there were his mum, his sisters, our immediate whānau, his school whānau. It was all happening. The Henderson branch is small and everywhere you went you could hear the crying and feel the grief.

Laments rang out: 'We shouldn't be here. We shouldn't be here … Why didn't you listen to me? … I told you I'd come and get you.'

It was raw grief like I had never heard before.

TERRY CHOSE a beautiful casket with Māori carving designs. They started to dress him then, and by now it was getting pretty late. Everything so far had happened without a break, but even now I didn't try to speed things up. I just let them be.

It could have been exhausting being the person making everything happen, but having a job to do meant I didn't get overwhelmed by my feelings. It's much better to be doing something useful than just standing around waiting.

Eventually, that part was done and Luke was able to go home with his mother for the night. We asked everyone else to leave the house to the immediate family so they could have time together. And everyone respected those wishes.

But the next day, when we took him to the Glenora Bears clubrooms at Glen Eden, the sea of people that had assembled there was mind-blowing. And it was a powerful atmosphere because people's grief at the loss of their loved one and teammate was combined with anger and frustration over how he had died.

I could hear it as Luke was walked in. The various club and school groups did their haka and they were all different. There was a sad haka and there was a haka where you could hear the frustration that people were feeling.

It was good that we had a safe place like the clubrooms for people to vent all their feelings and where they could be let loose and contained at the same time. Only immediate family would be at the funeral, so this was everyone else's chance to say goodbye and they made the most of it.

That final night was special for many people. I hung back and let them pay their respects.

'Are you going to have some time with Luke?' said Kaiora.

'I've already had my time with him,' I said, and she told me later my expression was fierce, like anger, even though I wasn't angry.

'Okay, sweet as,' she said, but I hadn't finished.

'I had four straight hours with him. I don't need any more.'

Kaiora realised she had hit a sensitive subject and left it at that. But that was how my grief came out.

His funeral and everything else that happened were exactly how he would have wanted. It paid tribute to all aspects of his short life: full-on for culture, full-on for manaakitanga; young people were involved as well as old. It was intensely sad and beautiful. So the tangihanga started in Auckland, at the clubrooms, all driven by the young people. We had the pōwhiri where we took him on, then the rest of the Māori protocol with the welcome, karakia and speeches. Once those formalities were over, it was open to anyone and everyone – female, male, young, old – to stand and kōrero or waiata.

The occasion took on a life of its own. I sat there and watched it all go on in front of me. Someone would get up and maybe not say anything at all but just sing a song. Then a group of boys would get up and do a haka. Then someone from the club would speak, and so on. But the main thing was that everyone got the opportunity to do what they wanted. No one was restricted as to what they could express, and no one had to rush because there was another funeral due in twenty minutes. That wouldn't have happened at the more formal tangihanga because the needs of the ceremony dictate what you can do.

Luke would have loved it.

Aunty Terry didn't want to blame anyone. The legal system would deal with things in time. For now, she just wanted to grieve.

She encouraged people not to be angry. At the funeral, you could feel an appetite for revenge simmering under. It was very strong. But Aunty Terry wasn't having it.

'I invite everyone here to share in mourning with us,' she told everyone. 'Please don't bring anger here. We want you to remember Luke for who he was.'

A lot of us were taken aback that she was able to express that at the time.

It went on all through the night and into the next morning. Then it was time to begin the drive north to lay him to rest in Ahipara. There was a finale in Auckland where everyone came to see him off at the clubrooms and say haere rā.

It seemed like everyone from the past few days was there to give him a farewell fit for a king. It was beautiful and magical. Scenes from these hours still turn up on my Facebook from time to time and I'm always stopped in my tracks by how special it was.

Once we got to Ahipara and the marae, we had to revert to tikanga and follow protocol. This was beautiful too but in a different way. There were a lot of people from Auckland in attendance. The manuhiri just kept coming and every time a guest arrived they were walked onto the marae formally. At the clubrooms, people just walked in and did what they felt like doing.

But the more formal arrangement also reflected Luke. The whole process covered all ways of thinking and grieving – from the new and informal to the traditional.

My uncle, Father Peter Tipene, conducted the Catholic service for Luke. It wasn't a mass, just prayers on the marae, but it was still very inclusive. And of course, there were plenty of people to sing so we had lots of hymns and waiata.

At the conclusion, we uplifted Luke's casket and everyone followed it on the walk to the cemetery about a kilometre away and he was buried next to his father.

HAVING TO CARE for one of my whānau in death was both the same as and different from doing it for anyone else. Certainly, the shock of a sudden death of someone close to you takes some time to settle down.

But I still had to do the same things I do for anyone else – organise the flowers, put a death notice in the newspaper.

I actually found it quite hard to move and get things done. Normally I'm quite tough on families about getting things done on time. For instance, the *Herald's* deadline for death notices is five o'clock but I never tell people that. I always say it is 4.30 and I want it by four.

But in Luke's case – when I was the one who had to do things – I found it really hard to get going. I couldn't work out what was wrong with me. *Why was I leaving everything to the last minute?*

Kaiora reminded me of it one day.

'Do you remember when Luke died and you were struggling to do things?'

'Yes – nothing was going right.'

'Oh, it was going right,' she said. 'You weren't going right.'

'What do you mean?'

'You remember the *Herald* notice?'

'Yes.'

'What were you doing?'

'I was trying to put the notice out.'

'And normally you take about ten minutes to do those but it took you three-quarters of an hour. And you tell everybody that they have to get their words to you by four o'clock and you were still writing it at four-thirty?'

She was right. I'd had all the words but I hadn't known what to say because this time it was my whānau. It was good for me to experience what families go through. I gained some understanding. It made me a bit more considerate of families when I'm asking them for details for the order of service sheets and the notices. I stopped hammering them to find the documents and get the photos they wanted and give me the information for the newspaper.

A month or so after Luke's tangi, I read an article about what had happened that night. Then it all hit me and I got really upset. I let it all out.

'I'm just remembering what I had to endure, seeing the marks on Lukey,' I told Kaiora.

She suggested we get some help and have a karakia, but I just needed to talk about it together and she was a wonderful support to me.

It's still close to the surface, though. Just a few days ago, I took another body over to the Glenora clubrooms. One of the coaches had died, and he was going to rest there for a while. As I drove the hearse down, it all came back to me. This had been a sudden death too – a car accident – and everyone turned up to pay their respects. It is such a tight-knit club with an amazing sense of community. It looked and felt exactly the way it had when we took Luke there. Even Luke's mother, Aunty Terry, and his sister, Kristina, were there because they are involved with the club. It was as though Luke's funeral had been just the day before.

It's now a few years after his death, and I still look to Terry and Kristina for the example they have set. Kristina has a baby and is getting on with life. She still plays a lot of sport and every time she has any sort of achievement she dedicates it to her brother. They used to encourage each other tremendously and she's moved forward since Luke died. She didn't give in to alcohol or drugs or any of the other things people use to help them through tragedies.

And her mum is the same staunch person. She has accepted the blow and moved on.

MY STAFF WERE wonderful too. As usual. They turned up and took over so I had some time to do a little grieving myself. I got to be on the receiving end of their skills. It was reassuring to learn how well our families are looked after during grief.

Taku manu ka turua ake nei,
he kāripiripi, he kāeaea

———————————

May you fly, my bird,
glancing restlessly as you dart about,
swooping like a hawk

Above St Gabriel's Church and urupā in Pawarenga. This is where Francis's pop is buried.

Left Two-year-old Francis in the kitchen at Nan and Pop's, Pawarenga.

Above Kaiora's siblings after pig hunting, at home in Puapua. There's still no electricity or phone coverage there.

Below Left Kaiora (back row, far right) with her parents and all her siblings in 1993.

Below Right Nine-year-old Kaiora and her sister Apikera outside their homestead in Kaitaia.

Above Left Little Francis.

Above Right Francis with his younger sister Moana.

Below Pop, Francis and Nan with our friends Jade and Te Arahi Maipi, at home in Pawarenga.

Above Nan (centre) with Francis's dad, also called Francis, and step-mum Debbie at the party for Nan and Pop's 80th birthdays.

Below Left Nan, Pa Patera and Francis's mum, Helen, at Pa Patera's ordination.

Above Newborn Francis in the arms of his proud dad, 1983.

Above Christmas in Pamapuria: Francis and all his cousins with Nan and Pop.

Below Left Our wedding day at the registry office in Kaiata. We couldn't afford rings so we just held hands. And then a good friend stood up and gave Francis a ring from her finger. 'Give this to your wife,' she said.

Below Right Pop spoilt his grandkids and gave them all too many lollies. Here he is with Mihaka.

Left The role of a funeral director: rain, hail or sunshine, you stand in a place where the bereaved family can see you. It is your duty to be aware of everything that is going on.

Below Francis was the lead funeral director at the funeral for Nona's dad, Stan Bakulich.

Left When we started out, we could only afford to stock three caskets at a time. Moronai, Nikora and Francis in 2010.

Left Francis with Logan Tipene (no relation) positioning our first lot of casket displays.

Left Nikora, dressed in his suit and polishing a casket.

Above Tragedy can bring out the best in people. In 2017, our community came together to bury a baby who had been abandoned in Mangere.

Below Buying our first hearse for the new Onehunga branch – the number plate is T4NGI.

Above To obtain your funeral director qualifications, you have to be assessed on casket lifting and hearse washing.

Below When your husband tries to educate you on how to wash a hearse – and then the babies get involved …

Mahi with the kids: Mihaka (above) helping Dad choose a new desk on Trade Me and, a few years later, rolling on the ground with Mikae during karakia; Francis multi-tasking (below), looking after Francis Jr and a casket at the same time.

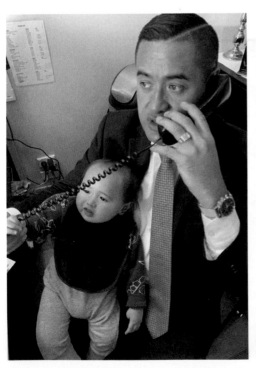 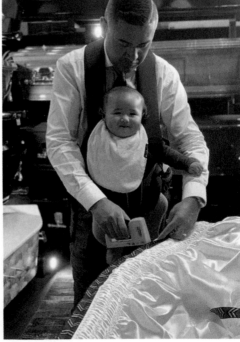

Left Nikora and Francis at Auckland International Airport, waiting for clearance to uplift a body. It was the first time Nikora went with Dad on the job.

Left One am: Dad had finally finished mahi and was so happy to come home to Mikae, who was just two weeks old.

Below Nikora, Mikae and Moronai during a tangi.

Left Nona, Kaiora and Francis, with the first hearse and casket to be driven through the newly built Waterview tunnel in Auckland; it was a special request from the deceased's family. Mrs Copeland was then repatriated to Samoa.

Left Kaiora with her mum (second from left) and some friends at the opening day of Tipene Funerals Onehunga, 2016.

Below Left The singing funeral director! Francis on *Homai Te Pakipaki*, Māori TV, accompanied by our nephew Lync Hetaraka.

Below Right Francis and Moronai at our annual Halloween party, 2013.

Whānau time. Francis (above) with his dad and our boys in 2018, before Francis Jr was born. It was the first time we went overseas as a family. And (below) on holidays with Haimona (second from right) in Rotorua, 2017.

Above Left Our first Christmas off, at Tokerau Beach in 2016 with our caravan.

Above Right Happy New Year, 2017.

Below Left We love going bike riding at Onehunga Bay Reserve.

Below Right Francis and Mihaka at Cape Reinga.

Above Francis paying his respects to his cousin Luke Tipene.

Below Mikae, Francis, Nikora and Moronai at Lukey's gravesite.

Our first pic together (top left). Little did we know then that one day we'd have five kids together, be the winners at the NZTV Awards 2019 of the Best Original Reality Series (for the second year in a row) and Best Māori Programme, and go on our future dates in a hearse. Lol.

CHAPTER ELEVEN

THE CASKETEERS

I NEVER WANTED to do *The Casketeers*.

The TV producer Annabelle Lee-Harris knew us because she had followed us some time ago when we were with Waitakere Funerals. She did a little story on Māori funeral directors for *Native Affairs* and she and my wife had stayed friends ever since. They had been texting each other.

'Would you be interested in us doing a TV show on you guys?' Annabelle asked one day. 'Like *Keeping up with the Kardashians* but with funerals.' And she said it would have humour at the centre of it – the humorous angle was there right from the start.

'What do you think, Francis?' said Kaiora, after she had filled me in on the basics. Obviously, with 'Finalist on *Homai te Pakipaki*' on my CV, it wouldn't have been my first experience in front of the TV cameras. But this was quite different.

'No, no, no,' I said. 'Absolutely not.'

I said no a lot of times. I didn't think people would want to see it anyway. About the only time you saw funerals or funeral directors on TV was if there was an important funeral being shown on the news.

But Annabelle kept talking to Kaiora about it.

'How would it look?' Kaiora wanted to know.

'Leave it to me. It will be fine,' said Annabelle.

My wife thought it was a bit of a joke. We wondered why anyone would want to make a programme like that, let alone watch it.

At the time, for some people, putting a notice on social media for their loved ones was still a no-no. That was going too far in public. But others were slowly accepting these kinds of changes and allowing them to be aired.

I kept saying 'No' for at least another year. I didn't think it would look right. I was just being a funeral director. But maybe attitudes changed in all the time I had been saying no, because eventually I said yes.

A crew came in – just a camera and a sound person – and followed us around for two days.

And as luck would have it, not long after they arrived, we got a funeral in.

'I just have to go and get a body,' I said, excusing myself.

'Can you ask them if we can come with the camera?' said Annabelle.

'No.'

'Please – just ask them?'

'Nooooo.'

But I did and it was okay with them. They were whānau and they were quite happy about it because they trusted us. They filmed me doing a karakia with the loved one before removing the body. I was in the middle of the prayer when the phone rang.

'Oh, that might be God ringing in and saying, "Hang on,"' I said, and everybody laughed.

At another point, I was calling Fiona from our staff Princess Fiona, after the character in *Shrek*. She didn't like it but it was all caught on film and when we watched it together she laughed.

So they not only had a real funeral, they had the humour they wanted in there as well. And alongside that they managed to capture some of those special sacred moments that are also part of the process. When it came to the part where we picked the body up, I thought it was so beautiful. And then they played music while we were driving off and that was beautiful too. It struck me that I had never seen anything like it on TV before, so I was happy to be part of it.

Over the two days they managed to collect all sorts of little moments and the production team ended up totally in love with it. Although it was only ever going to be a pilot to persuade someone to buy the show, a lot of the elements that people would love most about *The Casketeers* were already there in those first two days.

They brought it to us to have a look at when it was done. Kaiora was a bit nervous, which was only natural. She hadn't been the centre of a TV programme before. But she had a lot of trust in Annabelle. And we watched it and thought it was cool. They had music in the background – 'Tūtira Mai Ngā Iwi'.

And it didn't seem awkward at all. We liked it.

There was only one tiny bit I wasn't happy with – but I do have a way of letting small details bug me. In this case, it was how at the end of the pilot they got me to say: 'I'm Francis. I'm the boss. This is my funeral home and this is Tipene Funerals.'

At the time, I didn't mind it and other people liked it, but later I thought: *People know I'm the boss. I shouldn't have to say it.*

Annabelle took the finished product to Great Southern Television and they took it to TVNZ, who said they wanted it.

Making the first season wasn't hard at all. Because it was all new, there were no time restrictions.

The crew hung out with us for three months prior to filming. They left their cameras behind and came along on funerals, ate with us and got to know our personalities. So by the time we began for real, they knew exactly what was what and all the staff were used to having them around. When they turned the cameras on, everything felt perfectly natural and we trusted them. From the director to the sound person and the camera operator, they knew all our goofy ways and we knew theirs. It was just like having friends around.

They have all been wonderful to work with and it's been great to have the same team all the way through: our wonderful director, Susan Leonard, her producer sister, Carmen, our cameraman, Tom Walsh, and Wendy Adams doing the sound. They were all so sensitive and subtle.

When our show won Best Original Reality Series at the TV awards that year, it was awesome, and a big surprise as we were up against some high-powered shows. I was as happy for the production team as I was for Kaiora and myself.

It was just as well we all got on, because all of what we do and who we are was being put in the team's hands. They could possibly make or break our business, and by the time anyone found out it would be too late.

They wouldn't let us see any of it before it went to air. And they still don't. They said I wouldn't like it and would want to keep changing things, and they would never get it finished. And they were absolutely right.

They wouldn't even let us see the promos. We had a bit of marital discord over the first one when we saw it. It had me saying: 'I love my wife but I don't like working with her.'

'Oh no,' said Kaiora. 'Why did you say that?'

I couldn't even remember saying it. She took it personally but it was out of context and not nearly as bad if you heard everything else I said around it.

The night the first episode went to air, we sat in our seats gripping each other's hands. And straight after the news, Peter Williams said: 'And that's the news for January 13th, 2018. Coming up, *The Casketeers*.'

That meant it was really happening. We were so nervous.

But overall it was okay. Pop got to see it and I'm so glad because he died two days later. He told me it was too short.

Now when I watch it I don't have too many regrets. The things I worry about aren't the things about Kaiora and me. I worry about what the other funeral directors will think. Families and regular viewers won't pick these things up, but my colleagues will. They will be judging how I do everything and the procedures I follow and thinking to themselves: *I can't believe how he parked the hearse there*, and *Will you just look at how he's left that trolley crooked?* I think I'm always going to feel like that.

I know I make life harder on myself by having to check on things all the time. But when you are like this, it's even harder to be any other way. I've learned to live with myself, and Kaiora is a very patient person.

When they turned the cameras on, everything felt perfectly natural and we trusted them. From the director to the sound person and the camera operator, they knew all our goofy ways.

SO THE FIRST SERIES went out in New Zealand and we knew people liked it. But we didn't know the show was going to be on Netflix until we heard about it through the media. Before that, apart from screening on TVNZ, we had only been on Air New Zealand's inflight entertainment system, where we were put in the comedy section. I wonder how many people got caught out by that.

We didn't even have Netflix at home at the time. But from December 2018, we were being streamed to just about everywhere in the world. We went from a potential audience of a few million to a potential audience of everyone who can watch Netflix, which is a couple of hundred million people. Even then, we had no idea what that would mean.

First came the phone calls. People from the other side of the world rang us up for a chat. They forgot that it was the afternoon there and two in the morning here. And if we reminded them they just said that's okay they didn't mind, and kept on talking.

There was nothing we could do about that. The first rule of funeral directing is that people have to be able to contact you at all times, so, as I've mentioned, a funeral director's phone number is always going to be somewhere in the ads. It's unusual to be able to just pick up the phone and call someone you see on TV and I think that may have been behind a lot of the calls.

Some people were very insistent and would only talk to me. And they would try to fool Kaiora by saying they were my aunty and came from the same marae. We knew that wasn't true. But sometimes they got me on the phone and would be crying like I was Justin Bieber, saying: 'I've finally gotten through to you.'

There were no nasty ones. Most people were nice and just ringing to say hello and tell us they loved the show. There were a few who wanted to use our services. 'Would you travel this far and look after me when I pass away?' They genuinely thought our business was portable.

Most of them were Americans, but that included a high percentage of Hawaiians, presumably because of the Polynesian element.

We got regular fan mail too. There were long emails from people saying how grateful they were for who we are and for being able to learn about our culture. They felt connected with us when they saw a tangihanga. The karanga and the haka gave them goosebumps and they wanted the same kind of send-off.

We have had people land at Auckland Airport and drive straight to the funeral home in Onehunga to take a photo of themselves in front of the building.

Once, Kaiora was walking to her car when some people pulled up, yelling with excitement: 'There she is. There she is. Hello. We've just landed from LA and we just wanted to say hello.'

She was at the PostShop up the road when a girl behind her in the line put her hands on her and turned her around.

'You are much more beautiful in person,' said the girl.

'Hi,' said Kaiora.

'I'm so sorry,' said the girl, who had her phone out and was filming by now. 'I'm from Melbourne and I just needed to show my mum you're a real person.'

'Hi,' said Kaiora again.

There were a lot of moments like this but thankfully, after the first wave, they slowed right down. It was amazing how quickly being a celebrity got boring.

*

I LIKE IT when we are filming the show on a day when there is a funeral, because the crew can't interrupt us. We can't ask the cemetery attendants to take the coffin out and put it in again so the crew can get a better shot.

But it's a different matter in the funeral home, where they can have more control. 'Can you do that again? Can you just come back here and repeat that?' I understand that's what you have to do sometimes to make things look their best, but I prefer it when I can get on with things and the job comes first and TV second. I have to follow around after them putting the candles back in their right place and readjusting the drapes and all the other things they rearrange to get a better shot.

When we signed on, I never expected it to be a success. I thought it would be a simple documentary that a few people would watch and most people wouldn't. I wasn't expecting a reality TV show.

Not that I have anything against reality shows. I love *Married at First Sight*. Someone once suggested we could combine their format with ours, but I'm not sure the public is ready for *Buried at First Sight*. I know I'm not.

We were also surprised that the families whose tangi are shown on the programme all agreed to take part when we asked them. Only one refused in the first series. The others seemed to think it would be a nice memorial for their loved one. They wanted people to know who their mother or husband or daughter was. We had a few more say no in the second series. Most said yes straight away, but others just didn't want to share that much with the world.

'We love the show,' they said, 'but can we not be filmed, please?' I think some people saw the first season and remembered the funny stuff and were scared they might be made a mockery of. We were always happy to respect their wishes.

I've been told other funeral directors think it is good for the industry as whole. It normalises it and has made a lot of people more comfortable with it.

It's certainly been good for us as a business, but that has been a mixed blessing too. When the first season was first on, there was a big increase in business and enquiries. After a few months, it began to tail off. Then, after a quiet period, the second series began, and we got busy again. That made it hard for us to plan. Funeral directing isn't supposed to be a seasonal business like apple picking. We had to choose between taking on more staff in the busy times, who wouldn't have much to do in the quiet times, or trying to struggle through with the existing staff. We chose the second option, because we have great staff who can handle challenges, but it's stressful.

Overall, though, the business has grown and we give thanks to *The Casketeers* for helping that to happen. We weren't sure how much longer we would want to keep doing it but we committed to a third series. That was arranged to give us more breaks during filming, which made things easier.

There were some things Kaiora wasn't happy about in series two and we have tried to fix those for series three. She thought the scenes of me buying a suit or talking about my tummy operation made me look spoilt. And she felt there was too much of her complaining about me and not enough about her being an equal partner who makes decisions in the business. We have addressed those issues.

The humour is the thing people talk about most in the show, but sometimes I'm not sure exactly what they mean.

Also, because of the humour in the show, often when people see me on the street they look at me and say, 'You're the funeral guy,' and laugh. I don't think the kids like that so much.

When I watched the show, there were some things that people laughed at that I didn't find funny. I don't think the leaf blower is funny. I think it's a helpful tool. I didn't find lighting a match to get rid of the smell of poo funny. I think that is practical.

But the humour means that when people come up to me on the street they are smiling. I never thought that would be the reaction. I guess the TV people have done a good job to make it light-hearted and not too heavy.

The show has definitely affected how people react to me. I answer a lot of the night calls because I'm the boss and I know it's hard to work properly when you've had interrupted sleep. I want my staff to be at their best during the day so I go out at night when I can.

You really don't want to spend any more time out in the middle of the night than is necessary. But there is a problem with doing night removals now, which is that people are distracted because they have seen me on TV. 'It's him! He's here.' And they stand there gawking at a time when that's the last thing I would be thinking about.

It's awkward. I don't want to look stuck up. But I need to look and act professional. And I need to be warm at the same time. I've developed this little half-smile – not too much, not too little – but I think it needs more practice. Otherwise I'll just end up looking weird.

One part of our lives that you don't see on the show is our family. We have kept the children out of it as much as possible, although now Nikora is working for us you sometimes see him in series two doing jobs like washing cars.

The kids' reaction to the show has changed between the first two series. At first, they were very excited: 'Hey look – it's Mum and Dad on TV.' But pretty soon that turned into: 'Oh, no – it's Mum and Dad on TV again.' They're more likely to have a laugh at us than anything. And the smaller ones don't know any different, so they just carry on playing like nothing is happening. I think with social media, kids these days take it for granted that everyone is on TV in one way or another. No big deal.

It might be a bit different at school for the older ones. I know they get singled out for attention because of it. I asked Moronai if he minded and he said it was okay, as long as people didn't think that was all he was about. I know how he feels.

When they do mind is if we are out and people start asking for photos. Once again, it was different with the first series. There was the novelty value and everyone thought it was a bit of fun being treated like a celebrity. But it's amazing how quickly you get tired of that, especially if you are eating out at a restaurant. Now when it starts, our kids just want to get home as quickly as possible. That's fair. A lot of people don't understand that kids sometimes want Mum and Dad to themselves. Especially if their parents are busy mums and dads who work long hours.

Also, because of the humour in the show, often when people see me on the street they look at me and say, 'You're the funeral guy,' and laugh. I don't think the kids like that so much. Neither do I. I think: *Do you guys remember the beautiful, sad bits I really love?* We work hard to do justice to people's tangi every time one is shown in the programme. The humour comes from us; the funerals are always serious and I think they come across as very moving.

People also think they are entitled to an opinion on Kaiora's and my relationship. I wasn't expecting that. They often tell me I should listen to my wife more.

The other reaction to the show that surprises me – and it's one I get a lot – is when people say: 'I love how gentle you are and the way you handle the bodies.' How do people think we act? I think all funeral directors do that. It's our business to care for the dead. And that means being a caring person. If we aren't caring, we won't be in business very long. Perhaps some people have had bad experiences. It always makes me sad when I hear of that happening, because you only have one funeral.

I have always liked seeing funeral directors on TV myself. I can compare styles and pick up tips. Usually it's only when there is a funeral on the news, but I can see what others are wearing.

And what people do differently.

I loved the funeral for Cocksy the TV builder, because his casket had hammers for the handles and they put him in an old car and did a burnout on a field as part of the ceremony. I thought that was so great.

WE'VE BEEN SURPRISED at the different kinds of feedback the show gets from people around the world. But death is one experience all humans have in common and that has obviously helped us reach all sorts of different people.

We didn't just get reviews in the TV pages of newspapers. Funeral directors' websites also took an interest and their responses were as funny as anyone else's, like this one from connectingdirectors.com, which is based in the US, that said the show 'leads the perception of the funeral director FAR away from the dark-and-morbid stereotypes and towards a far more relatable character with the same silly jokes, struggles, and insecurities as the average person'. It called me 'an exuberant and delightfully eccentric funeral director who loves cleaning, singing, and irritating his wife in that cute-angry kind of way'. That reviewer was a funeral director who also pointed out our show and business weren't typical because 'most funeral directors are not going to sing, play guitar and dance at a funeral'.

Well, I don't dance and it's not my fault if other funeral directors haven't learnt to play the guitar.

Australian dailyreview.com described *The Casketeers* as 'a poignant, funny and often revelatory look at the inevitability of death, and what we can learn from the people so intimately connected with it', which was nice. But they also called me 'a loveable busybody'.

E tupu, e hua, e ohu e te anuhe

———————————

**As a person's importance increases,
so too do those who seek their favour**

CHAPTER TWELVE

PUBLIC LIFE

THE DOWNSIDE of the exposure that comes with being in a TV show is that people who watch it assume we are exactly the way we appear on TV. They don't realise they are seeing only a tiny part of our lives – literally a few hours out of an entire year. It's not meant to be the whole story.

You can't win sometimes. For instance, I once tried hard *not* to get any publicity for something but still couldn't avoid it. It was when I heard about the case of a woman called Eramiha Pairama.

Her son had been killed in a logging accident. The company he worked for had been ordered to pay reparations, but it went into liquidation and she didn't get a cent, which meant she couldn't afford a headstone that she dearly wanted to provide for her son. Kaiora and I read about her situation and it touched both our hearts. My wife urged me to make contact.

I had read about it on the stuff.co.nz website, so I called them anonymously, asking to be connected with Eramiha. We were put in touch through her lawyer and she turned out to be a lovely woman.

'Look, dear,' I said, 'we have a spare headstone. It's a nice green pounamu with a nice base. Come and have a look. You might not like it, but it is yours if you do.'

She jumped at the chance and said yes.

But then it all got a bit tricky. Two things can happen when you do a good deed. One is that the people are very happy, which happened in this case. But the other is that you can be seen as seeking more attention from the public: 'Oh look – they haven't got enough glory yet.'

I wanted our names to be kept out of it, but someone let it out that it was 'The Casketeers' who were providing the headstone. I was embarrassed, but I am still happy we were able to help.

People also see the nice cars and the Rembrandt suits on TV and decide they are entitled to have an opinion about that. 'Those people must be up themselves because they have a good car.' Or 'Why doesn't he just buy a suit from Hallensteins?' And 'Is that what their customers are paying for?'

My answer to that is always that how we present ourselves is a mark of respect for the loved one. I think if I wore track pants all the time and drove a ute everywhere, our business would suffer and there would be plenty of negative comments about that.

I like nice clothes, maybe because I didn't have a lot of new clothes when I was growing up. And social media has tricked me. I once bought some new clothes online and suddenly I was getting lots of messages from Google: 'Hi Francis. We thought you might like to try these clothes.' It goes shopping for me and then it tells my Facebook page. I couldn't work out how it knew me so well, then I found out it was the computer at work.

'You know Google can understand what you do, don't you?' said Kaiora.

'What do you mean?'

'It follows you to see what you're interested in and then tries to sell you things like that.'

I was astonished. There is just no privacy any more.

I also give in to temptation more because now I can buy regular clothes. When I was a lot bigger, I had to buy special big-boy clothes, which are more expensive. My clothes now are much more affordable. I am not a big person looking for clothes that will make him look thin.

I used to have to have special suit fittings for work clothes.

'Do you know what the purpose of a suit is, Francis?' asked a man who was fitting me once.

'To make you look neat and tidy?' I said.

'Yes, that's one thing, but the main purpose of a good suit is to make you look smaller than you are.'

'My goodness. How does that work at 140 kilos?'

'It's all in the shaping.'

I put a suit on and he demonstrated where the suit needed to go in and out to make me look good. I wasn't convinced but I did know black was slimming, so I ordered two plain black suits. Patterns are no good because they can blow you up like a balloon.

I like to look presentable and I like my staff to be able to look the same. I was hurt by an online comment that said: 'he dresses himself up and doesn't care what his staff look like', because that's not true.

Kaiora and I spend a lot of money on our staff and try to help them look good. But the difference between them and me is that I can't force them to wear stuff if they don't like it.

The funeral director
is supposed to be the
person on the move at
a funeral, ducking in
and out of people and
getting everything done
unobtrusively. It was very
hard to be 140 kilos of
unobtrusive.

We have bought beautiful suits from Working Style and other top men's fashion labels for our male colleagues Logan and Stan, because I wanted everyone to look equally good.

It wasn't anything loud – just a light-grey suit with some square patterns on it and some polka dots. But they said it wasn't them. You put them in a black or dark brown suit and they love it.

Also, I live in suits. I have lots of shorts and T-shirts but no time to wear them except to bed. I could wear them on the weekend, if I had a weekend. But just about every Saturday and Sunday, I am at work in a suit. So I need to have several. I like to change them and I don't wear the same one two days in a row because they have to get a chance to breathe and they need to be hung up for a while to get their shape back.

I ALSO GOT a lot of comments on how I had lost so much weight between the first and second *Casketeers* series. I didn't really *lose* the weight. I know exactly where it went, because I had it taken away with a gastric sleeve operation.

Obesity is a problem in my family and in my culture, with many Māori suffering health problems because of their weight.

Eating has always been a big temptation for me. I don't want it to be a temptation for others too, so if I eat bad food in the office I do it away from the staff. I try to set a good example and encourage them to eat healthily. But the food I really like is KFC, which I still have now and again. Because my stomach is smaller now, one drumstick is enough. After that I'm bloated.

The other big problem is bread. I've told everyone I'm giving up bread, but it's so hard. It doesn't matter what kind. Any sort will do: normal shop bread, Māori bread, fried bread. I'm like an alcoholic for bread. I wish I knew what they put in it to make it so addictive.

I try to make up for my indulgence with lots of physical activity. If I can balance it out with a walk or bike ride, I feel better. Otherwise I fill up on bread, sit around and mope and I can feel the scales going up.

Finally – pies. I have a favourite bakery up north that makes a brand called Keri Pies. They have not too much pastry and a lot of meat, when a lot of pies are the other way around. But you can only find them in certain places. If we are travelling north, the craving for a Keri Pie gets stronger the further we go. It drives Kaiora crazy.

'Are there Keri Pies here?'

'No, darling.' And we keep driving.

'Do you think they might have Keri Pies here?'

'No, Francis.' And so on. If all else fails, there is one last shop before we get to Pawarenga and they nearly always have one, but I hate having to wait that long.

When I eat them now, even though I can't eat as many as before my operation, they take me back in memory to the feeling I used to get when I could eat as much as I want.

Pies were always my downfall. It was no wonder that I grew very big and finally had to do something about it. There was a vanity aspect to this and a health aspect.

For one thing, I was unfit and could have ended up extremely unwell. I have seen the long-term effects of being overweight from a young age.

Another problem with my size was that it made my job difficult. The funeral director is supposed to be the person on the move at a funeral, ducking in and out of people and getting everything done unobtrusively. It was very hard to be 140 kilos of unobtrusive. My job is to both be there and not be there. Well, I was definitely there. I could have blocked out the sun.

I got tired quickly from quite simple activities. At home, I complained to Kaiora: 'I'm too big for this job. I can't keep this up.'

She wasn't very sympathetic. 'Put the bread down and hit the road then,' she said. And I could see how that worked, because while I was busy eating and complaining, she was working and exercising to keep fit. She looked and felt great.

Nothing I tried worked, if it depended on willpower. Which is how I ended up looking into the surgery option. I had reservations about that. Mainly, I felt like I had copped out, like I didn't deserve to be slimmer because I hadn't done any work to get that way. Some people put a huge effort into losing weight, and they must really enjoy that sense of achievement, but anyone can go and get someone to cut a bit of their stomach out.

I look at the motivational groups on Facebook or Instagram and think how much more satisfying it would have been to do it the hard way. But then I might never have done it at all. It was a lot easier to do that than to get on a treadmill or change what I ate.

When people compliment me, I think, *Yeah, but it was only an operation. I didn't literally work my arse off.*

And now it is done, I have to work hard to keep it off. It can easily go back on. I got down to ninety kilos then went to a big whānau event and gained two kilos over one long weekend. I nearly got depressed but I made a big effort and got back to ninety again.

The plus side is that I feel better and have a lot more energy to do things with my family. When I was big and people told me what would happen if I lost weight, I honestly didn't believe them. It didn't seem possible. But it has happened and I am so grateful.

As for the vanity side of things, my problem was that I looked so … big. Recently, I saw a photo of Kaiora and myself that was used in publicity for the Henderson branch. I weighed my heaviest then and when I look at that photo now, I have to ask myself one question: *What the hell was I thinking?*

The operation was scary. I was warned about it in advance. I'm grateful my wife supported me through it.

'You're going to have pain here, here and here,' they told me before I went under. I didn't like the sound of any of that. The morphine and other tablets were all good to go when I woke up again. When I did, the doctor was there.

'Francis, hello. How is your pain on a scale from one to ten, ten being the highest?'

'Doctor, I don't have any pain. It's a one.'

'What?'

'Honestly – it's not sore at all. There's no pain. I think I'll go home now.'

This was just a few hours after the operation and the doctor was very firm.

'You can't go home yet,' he said, and that was that.

So I went back to sleep. When I woke up the doctor came back again.

'How is the pain from one to ten now?'

'It's a one. There is no pain.'

And there really wasn't. I hadn't even had any painkillers. It felt like the anaesthetic from the operation was still in there doing its job. And the next day when everything had finally worn off, there was a bit of bruising but that was perfectly manageable. What I really needed was food.

Eventually, they brought me a sort of chicken broth in a tiny cup. It looked a bit odd.

'What the hell is that going to do?' I said.

'Have a teaspoon,' said the doctor.

I did and it was so nice. It was like KFC, a pie and all my other favourite foods all combined into one thing. And after a little sip, I was so full. I felt like I would spew if I had any more.

That is when my new relationship with food started. This was amazing, that a little bit of something could fill me up.

There have been other benefits. I have sleep apnoea, which is a condition connected with being overweight. It means you stop breathing for short periods during sleep, and since my early twenties I have had to sleep with a machine that would start me breathing again when it happened.

The theory was that some of the weight I 'lost' would be fat from around my throat and that would let the airway open up. It worked, and now I can sleep for two or three hours without the machine. Before the operation, I would wake up choking if I was asleep that long.

The operation has changed my life in so many ways. But I still have to put in some effort to keep the benefits. A stranger reminded me about this when he came up and spoke to me at a function.

'Excuse me, sir,' he said, 'I saw you eating a pie on your TV show and you said you can't eat as much of the pie any more because the mind needed to have a hui with the stomach and they hadn't got on the same page.'

I cracked up, even though I couldn't remember saying it.

'I want my mind to have a hui with my puku as well,' he went on, 'because they're not talking to each other properly. One of them is overeating.'

The table was in fits. But that is the problem – those two parts have to work together. This part wants to eat all the time and the other part doesn't need it.

I think *The Casketeers* might have had something to do with our being at that function. We received an award even though we hadn't entered for it.

'You won't believe what's happened,' said Kaiora, coming off the phone one afternoon.

'Okay. What?'

'We've been nominated for the Māori Entrepreneurial Leader Award and we've won.'

And I said the F-word.

'What the F-word!' I said. 'Really?'

We got one of the 2018 University of Auckland Aotearoa Māori Business Leaders Awards and it was 'in recognition of building a successful business and through that being a role model for other Māori'.

It was so nice. The function was held at the university and we got to stay in a hotel in downtown Auckland.

We had been to the awards for three years in a row to mingle and enjoy all the glitz and glamour, but never thinking we would get anything. I thought it was only for past students who had done well. But it is not.

We didn't just go for the fun and the good kai but to be inspired by the successful people you see there. The year that I got most inspired was the year that Jason Witehira won. He owns the New World supermarket in Freemans Bay and I thought he was right out of our league. When he spoke about his business and the millions of dollars it turns over, I thought, *That's not us*. But we still felt inspired.

So when we actually won something, I was completely blown away. Never in my wildest dreams would I have imagined that.

Normally there is a process involved in being up for one of the awards. You can nominate yourself or get nominated, and then you have to do masses of paperwork about yourself and your business. But this year they just rang us three weeks before the night and told us we had it. So really we found out we'd been nominated and won in the same phone call.

Winning was nice but once again the mixing and mingling was the best part. Because of our 'fame', more people wanted to mix and mingle with us than in previous years. Which ended up being a bit embarrassing. We hadn't expected that, and we had invited some friends to come along to enjoy the night and so we wouldn't have to worry about running out of people to talk to.

It turns out when you take manuhiri, it can be awkward. People we didn't know kept coming up to us, taking photos, wanting to know about getting a TV series. We met people from all walks of life. That's why they go – in order to network. There were people offering us all sorts of products: 'If we give you some wine, maybe you could open the fridge door up to show it on the TV show.' People were offering us cheese to sell our families. I said: 'We're a funeral home, not a supermarket.' I wasn't going around asking people if they would like caskets.

To all those winemakers and cheesemakers, I said: 'I'll have to wait till you die to return the favour. It could be a long time.'

It's lucky there weren't any bakers there or I might have been tempted.

But it all meant we hardly had any time to share the moment with our friends.

'So when are you guys gonna come and sit with us?' they asked, and we tried to, but then there would be someone else barging in. In the end, we escaped to a little bar across the road so we could actually talk to the people we had invited.

Another thing I have noticed with these functions is that I am developing a taste for that style of food. It is not like the kai on the marae. *This doesn't feel very Māori*, I thought to myself the first few times. But now I really like it. It's fancy. You get an entrée, then a main and a dessert.

I used to wonder if it would be enough, because they are really small portions. But you do get full over three courses, if you take your time. That might change how we do things on the marae. We might stop putting out a mountain of food at functions. I'm getting quite used to these lovely dinners.

He toka tūmoana, he ākinga nā ngā tai

———————————

**A good leader is like a rock standing firm in the sea,
despite lashings by the tides**

CHAPTER THIRTEEN

THE SUPPORTING CAST

AT TIPENE FUNERALS, we have a company tradition of mutual support that has grown up naturally. When any of us has a tangi, the others are there to be their backbone and help them through.

When a death affects their immediate family, we get them on their way immediately, and we are behind them saying, 'What do you need?' We know what funerals are and we kick into gear. We will provide food. We will arrange a car. It's important that they don't have those extra worries and can focus on their families.

We tend to be pretty practical. There are the immediate requirements of death to deal with, but there are other practicalities as well. Maybe the person needs a loaf of bread and a bottle of milk at home. Maybe they would appreciate some sausages for a barbecue to feed all the manuhiri who are going to turn up.

Wherever someone has died, there will be people needing to be fed. I love how everyone gets stuck in and makes themselves useful. Donations and flowers are fine, but sausages are useful.

I know I can be a bit controlling or micro-manage-y. When my pop died, the staff were there for me, keen to help. But I wasn't used to getting help. I said I will do this and that and everything else there was to be done.

Afterwards, they complained that I hadn't let them help me.

'I understand now,' I said. 'I'm sorry. I accept your love. I accept your frustration at me now. It didn't feel right for you to do that for me, because I'm the boss and thought I could take care of everything.'

Fiona said: 'Sometimes you've got to stop being the boss and just step away and let us be your friend.'

It made me feel sad and good at the same time.

When Denise lost her dad, we saw how devastated she was and we responded. We did the same for her as she does for our families. He died in Whangarei, so we helped her get up there to uplift him, bring him back to Auckland, prepare him and then take him back up north.

BEING A FUNERAL DIRECTOR is not something you can do on your own. When you think about it, you need a bare minimum of two people to do the job – at least one to carry the head and another to carry the feet.

At Tipene Funerals, we are truly blessed to have a wonderful staff whānau. I think *The Casketeers* makes this clear.

My staff selection process is probably a bit different from that at other firms. To start with, we use social media networks and our Facebook page to let people know we are looking for someone. And of course, they send in their CVs and we have face-to-face interviews. The interviews are much more important than what's written on someone's CV. I employ people based on how I feel about them when I meet then. If their wairua is right, they will get a job even if they don't have much experience.

Someone could be well qualified and be the wrong person, or unqualified and the right person. If you're punctual and tidy already, you will probably go straight to the shortlist. After all, I had been working as a funeral director for years before I went and got a piece of paper to say I was qualified, so I can't expect anything different of other people.

The qualifications aren't so important because there are a lot of basic funeral director qualities we can teach on the job. And some important ones that can't be taught.

If you have some te reo Māori, that is a plus, because many of our people want a funeral to acknowledge their language. If you can lead a prayer for a group and aren't shy of big gatherings, that is a plus, because sometimes a minister might have got lost on the way to the service and if you can take care of things till they get there, that will keep things moving. And if you carry a bit of mana with you, that is a plus – because sometimes you might need to exert some authority to keep things in order.

If you can sing and play guitar, that is a big plus. Waiata is such a beautiful part of a tangi. Just about everyone knows the hymn 'Whakaaria Mai'. I love it. I think it has united us as a country.

So that is how we have assembled the people who work at Tipene Funerals. I've never really had to manage staff before, so I feel very lucky.

Everyone is here to support each other. All of us – including Kaiora and me – have our shortcomings. If there are things we are not so good at, someone else will be able to fill that gap. And we have our problems and dramas. When our last three babies were born, Kaiora and I had people on staff who are still with us and every time they said, 'Don't worry about anything. Take care of having the babies. We'll take care of the business.'

In funeral directing, it's not unusual for the babies to end up taking over the business. Many of the best-known New Zealand firms have seen several generations take their turn running things.

I am a fan of funeral directing as a family business – up to a point. I love a husband and wife doing it. I love the stories of the Littles and the Morrisons and others.

But based on my short experience in the industry, I wouldn't employ too many of my own family. I'd probably take on a select few, and they might not be blood relatives but related by marriage.

I have several reasons.

If we ever have a falling-out in the firm, I wouldn't want that to lead to a permanent rift in the family. Whānau comes first.

Also, I have employed multiple members of one family, with the result that when there has been a death in that family, they all head off to the funeral and we are left short-staffed.

There are also lots of administrative aspects to the business that Kaiora and I share but that I wouldn't want out in the wider family.

I know if the business keeps growing, there will come a time when there is too much management for us to handle on our own, and then there will be some tough decisions to be made. We still share the dream of a small business that just the two of us could manage together, so maybe we will downsize. And the minute either of us started to fall out of love with the work we would have to reconsider things.

Being a funeral director is not something you can do on your own. You need a bare minimum of two people to do the job – at least one to carry the head and another to carry the feet.

But at the moment, I have responsibility to my staff and their families, who need to eat and pay rent. I wouldn't change the team I have for the world. They are like family anyway.

THERE ARE A LOT of other people involved in every funeral we do who aren't on our staff: sometimes the police or the coroner; the freelance embalmer; the GP who was seeing the deceased; and the cemetery staff.

Secular celebrants are becoming a popular choice to conduct funeral services, but I think they are more likely to be found conducting Pākehā funerals. Māori and Pacific Island families usually want some sort of religious component, so there will be a member of the clergy involved at some stage.

Because I grew up Catholic, I have noticed that the Catholic approach to funerals has changed a lot. There used to be just entrance, homily, eulogies, finish. Now it's entrance song, photo presentation, musical item, release of the doves – they've opened up more to the way we are doing funerals these days. I let families know that if it's at a Catholic church there may be restrictions. But I always talk to the priest, and many of them will try very hard to meet the family's wishes.

We also work with staff at hospital morgues. Not everyone who dies in hospital goes to the morgue. Families or funeral directors can request a ward release, which most people are more comfortable with. Obviously, you have to be a bit sensitive when it comes to timing. You don't want to be uplifting a body when the other people in the ward are getting their rice pudding.

Hospitals now have better facilities for families than they used to. They have lounges where people can get together, and they make it easier for families wanting to see their loved ones before they go to a funeral director.

While funeral directors often have a faint niggle in the back of their minds about how long it is going to take for their account to be paid, cemeteries don't. They won't start digging the grave until it has been paid for in advance.

We used to pay for graves on behalf of families, but that was money we often never saw again, so we don't do that any more. Families must pay the day before the funeral at the latest or there won't be a grave there when the funeral arrives. Which is why you will find me on the morning of a funeral on the phone to a cemetery: 'Hello, it's Francis Tipene here. Just checking payment has been made for Mr So and So's grave?'

Cemetery staff are generally very helpful and accommodating, but there are some things even they can't do. A family once asked us to bury their mother upside down on their father so she was on top and they were face to face. It was what she wanted.

The cemetery said no. What if the lid gave way and fell out when she was put in the grave? They seemed to think it was a health and safety issue. I couldn't really see that. She was dead.

However, although lids are strong, we had never heard of anyone being buried upside down, so we didn't have any evidence that it wouldn't give way.

The family said, 'Why not strap the coffin shut?'

That seemed reasonable to me, although I wasn't sure how the mourners would react to hearing the thud of the body bouncing when we turned the casket over.

In the end, the cemetery won that argument and fortunately I've never been asked to bury someone upside down again.

Kia mau ki te tūranga o Taputapuātea

———————————

Hold fast to the ancient foundations of Taputapuātea

CHAPTER FOURTEEN

TWO TYPES OF TANGI

IT SHOULDN'T BE a surprise that funerals, and in particular tangihanga and Māori funeral practices, have become such a big part of my adult life. They were a big part of my childhood.

Many people from Pawarenga had migrated to Auckland for work and to build a better life over the years. But when they died, it was time to come home again. And that meant work for us. I'm sure most of the whānau in Auckland didn't understand how much preparation we had to do every time a tangi came north. Feeding people was a big part of it – in every sense. There was butchering the cows, lighting fires, gutting the pigs and sheep. Every available uncle and aunty turned up to help with the cooking.

As kids, we got given all the jobs we could manage. We didn't have to slaughter any animals, though we certainly took a keen interest in observing the process.

In fact, years later when I attended my first post-mortem and saw a human ribcage opened up, it immediately reminded me of all the animals I'd seen in the same state up north. I realised we look exactly like any other animal. So when I saw my first human,

I wasn't shocked at the sight; I was shocked that it looked so familiar.

Not long ago, a family member from Pawarenga died here in Auckland. The tangi was the same process as up north but different.

Everyone came together and played their part. We had a ceremony here in our chapel, prayers and mihi and then it was time for food. Instead of killing a sheep, we got Uber Eats. But we set the food out in just the same way as we would at a country tangi.

I'll be getting reimbursed for the Uber Eats, but back when I was a kid nobody had to pay for anything because nobody charged for anything. Someone would contribute a sheep, someone else would make the bread. Everyone did their bit and no one complained about the cost in money or time. I know there wasn't much else to do with your time up there, but there are people who will complain about anything.

I have a complaint about the pace of life – and death. Even though I earn my living as a funeral director in New Zealand's biggest city, I sometimes yearn for the slow pace and the quiet of the old days. We get so busy, it's easy to forget what the past was like. I think everyone should slow down and stop trying to conquer the world.

Maybe we should just get some bread, butter it and put jam on it instead of relying on takeaway. That might be more satisfying than getting someone else to do it.

And if we aren't careful, the day might come when there is a tangi to be held at Pawarenga and we can't find anyone who remembers how to kill a cow and feed the people.

I'm not a natural-born killer myself. If I was ever asked to slaughter a cow, the first thing I would have to do is ask for gloves. Nobody asked for gloves in Pawarenga. They did everything with a knife and their bare hands.

I was lucky to be exposed to that way of life when I was. It was another advantage of the way Nan and Pop brought me up.

It has been different for my children. The other night, my son Moronai was at a church activity where they killed a pig and served it. He was so excited, he rang us and told us what was happening. Then he sent us a picture of himself with the pig over his shoulders and I thought that was very cool.

Next minute, he was home again.

'Dad, they got all the guts out of the pig and I couldn't watch,' he said. He is eleven, which is probably the right age to be shocked by something like that if you haven't been prepared for it.

And that's when I realised my children haven't had a lot of the basic experiences that I take for granted. We had to have a talk about how meat works and what I was exposed to growing up. I explained exactly how those pork spare ribs he loves to eat get to his plate. I may have turned him vegetarian. But every generation learns from the previous one and teaches the next one in turn. That's the circle of life at work.

When you grow up with something, you don't think twice about it, no matter what it is.

For instance, on my Tongan side, we eat horse as a delicacy. Gutting a horse is another matter altogether. That's a big job. My two sides are at odds when it comes to how we treat horses. In Māori culture, horses are our friend and our vehicle. They are a tool we use to get to places and obtain food. They aren't the actual food. We would never dream of eating horse.

But in Tongan culture, horse is a delicacy – and you can buy it in south Auckland. It can be seen at Tongan funerals, and if the funeral has a royal connection you will be given some in a plastic container for you to take away and cook.

WHEN I WAS GROWING UP, it was Māori funerals that shaped most of my attitudes to tangi. It was the same for Kaiora. We learnt that when someone died, you dropped everything and headed for the marae. One minute things are going along smoothly and you are outside playing with your friends, then the phone rings and your aunty or uncle or a cousin has died. There are a few moments of eerie silence, then a big burst of activity. Normal life is put on hold until the tangi is over.

When I was a child, a tangi actually meant a good time. Nan kept us out of school and we enjoyed the great spirit that arose out of the community coming together with a single goal. And it meant our cousins who we hadn't seen in ages would be coming up north. So, in a strange way, it was something we enjoyed.

For those of us who were living up north there was a routine to follow. Once we knew what time the body was coming, we would organise the meat, decide what day to go over to the marae, find the linen for the wharenui – which Nan always worried about – and make a trip to Kaitaia to buy the extra food that would be needed to feed everybody.

Nowadays, a new generation does things differently. The tangi may be split into two parts – one in Auckland and the last bit up north. People don't just drop everything and leave their work and other commitments in town to go to a country tangi the way they used to. That used to create a lot of misunderstanding and conflict, especially between Pākehā bosses and workers and their Māori colleagues. Whereas the body used to rest on the marae for three days, now it might be only overnight. We did that with my own grandfather when he died.

We're very urbanised here in Auckland. At home, it was easy to just go to a tangi – here, you have to take leave. If you want to follow the old custom and head to the marae for three days, you can't just say, 'I'm off to a funeral.' You have to get a certificate.

The sentiment of tangihanga has remained, but the means to achieve it have moved with the times.

Traditions aren't set in stone. They have to change and adjust for people, otherwise they will be abandoned altogether.

Some traditions of tangihanga have been kept, some have been replaced and some have been updated, but all are alive in one way or another.

One of the least understood is tono, the tradition by which Māori, wherever they die or have lived their lives, are taken back to their ancestral marae for burial. This sometimes makes headlines when fights break out between marae with competing aims. There are legal battles and stories of body-snatching, and they are nearly always overblown and often simply not true. Tono is such an established practice that ways have been developed to settle disagreements without too much fuss. But the disagreements still happen.

The big picture is that if a body is lying in state and people come along to request that it be taken to a certain marae, that is seen as a great honour – all these people coming to ask for your body are giving credit to your mana.

Sometimes I have been present at these discussions in connection with my own whānau and had to calm things down when they started to get heated.

But when things go as they should, there will be a big kōrero and all sides will get to take part in the debate and have their arguments heard. Beautiful words will be spoken and you often learn more about the person at this part of the process than at any other time.

It is a time of reflection and deep thoughts. Sometimes I think three days might not be enough because there are some big decisions that need to be made.

When someone comes to tono for a body, they will get up and acknowledge the whare, the mate and everyone who is gathered there. Then they will go on to a whakapapa, which is where a lot of learning is. In the genealogy, they will try to link the deceased person to the marae where they want them to go. And they will probably dress it up with some beautiful stories and words about experiences this person has had to do with this marae. People are often spellbound to hear all these new things about the person.

And then someone else will stand up and say, 'Let me tell you this other whakapapa and how he is connected to his other marae.' Tangihanga is like a university. You not only learn about whakapapa and strands of different iwi and hapū, you might also learn how you fit into the picture: 'Oh that's my tūpuna. I know that person.' Or, 'I never knew he was connected to that person.'

It may be the first time you hear about a wife or two you didn't know he had. That can be a very interesting learning experience.

At the same time, a decision needs to be made by the family. The people who wanted the body to go north might change their minds after hearing from the people who want it to go south. They might not have known there were links to the southern marae. If you let your loved one go to a marae you are not familiar with, then it establishes links between you and that marae too, because your loved one is buried there and you will always go back there and visit.

High-profile cases like that of Billy T James are very much exceptions. I feel sorrow and aroha for the families who went through that.

People need to be happy with the solution they go away with at the end. After all, they will have to live with it for the rest of their lives.

Of course, if the person has written down what they want to happen, it's a bit more difficult. But even then, there can be compromise.

I had a case where a man had said he wanted to be buried at a marae up north where his wife was buried. Everyone was happy with that. But then whānau from down the line arrived and they had a different opinion. 'Mum and Dad are both from up north,' they said, 'but one of his legs is from down the line.' That's how they put it in their oration. Left arm down there, right arm there, other arm over there.

He had a connection to their marae down the line, and they were saying if he was buried up north, the rest of the family would have nothing to connect them to the south. They needed to maintain that link between people in the whakapapa.

The family talked about it and decided not to follow the instructions he had left but to send him south. He was dead.

They were the ones who had to do everything. They had the final say.

And in the long run, it would be the best of both worlds: Mum would be up north, keeping the link there, and Dad would be down the line. Mum and Dad wouldn't be together but, said the family, they could be together in heaven. They didn't need to be together in the ground. And this new generation would have two homes. That shows how good it is to be open to words and suggestions. That's how this family learnt so much.

Another thing we have in Māori process is kawe mate, which is caring for the dead, not physically but spiritually. For example, in that case of the family changing their mind, because the matua wasn't going up north physically, he would be taken there symbolically.

The ceremony is the same as if his body was actually there. He will be called on. There will be a pōwhiri, with a photo of him at the front. Speakers will talk about whakapapa and his connections to that place. They will probably express their dismay that he is not being buried there, but they will thank the manuhiri for bringing his spirit with them. And the event will finish with kai to break the tapu. Kawe mate is not a very well-known tradition, but it is still strong.

Another tradition that is being altered somewhat is that of the immediate family of the dead person not eating during the days of the tangi. When you are in tangihanga mode, you are tapu because you are carrying the sacredness of the event. We finish a tangi with a big kai not because we are hungry (although we probably are, especially me) but because the ritual of eating clears the tapu and puts us back in the state of noa. We are ready for life

Every generation learns from the previous one and teaches the next one in turn. That's the circle of life at work.

again. We have come out of the space of pō and back to the world of light.

When a family have been grieving and showing their love for the one who has died, and they have done so with no food in their stomachs, eventually they run out of tears. When that happens, it means they are ready to move on to the next stage of life. They have something to eat in order to mark that. Only the living eat. They are so drained that they just need to rest, get some nutrition and gain some energy to keep going. I think the symbolism of eating and not eating is very beautiful.

Nowadays, it is a bit more difficult to go without food for that long. There are practical obstacles. There may be children or other people who need to eat because they have diabetes or some other illness. So now a lot of wharenui have a little room out the back, with a kitchen and shower, put there specifically for the immediate family to use during the tangi. They can eat, but they will eat by themselves and not come into the main dining room, just so they can uphold the tapu.

WHEN THERE IS A FUNERAL in Māoridom, everything comes out. I might have a bone to pick with my late uncle or aunt, and this is my last chance to do something about it. During the time of tangihanga, we put our raruraru – our differences – aside and we focus on what is important to us. People who didn't like the dead person will still show up to pay their respects or say, 'You were a mongrel – remember when we were young and you stole this or did that and I'll never forgive you and I hope you go to hell.' Sometimes they praise and condemn the person in the same kōrero. And they will often come a long way to do it.

I think this is one of the great strengths of tangihanga, that these things can be brought out and dealt with. You wouldn't do that in a mainstream funeral. Then it's only beautiful words allowed.

But following some sharp words at a tangi, words of love and comfort will come and, because of what went before, they will be so deep and meaningful that they move you to tears. My emotions will get a real workout at a tangi. My wife will tell you I'm a stubborn hua, and my staff will tell you I can be a bit of a prick of a boss. And they are both right.

But I'm softer than anyone I know and cry very easily if something makes me sad. That is what this industry does – it tests my patience, provokes my anger and brings out so much emotion.

I believe that all these sides to Māori funeral practices mean we can deal with and resolve our grief as soon as possible but without rushing it or treating it lightly.

A lot of mainstream funeral homes employ counsellors. Personally, I quite like the idea. But it isn't part of Māori tradition. The first time I heard about it was when I went to my funeral director's training course in Wellington.

With the Māori way, people are not left hanging at the end of a funeral, wondering why they feel so bad. From the death itself, to the dressing, arrangements, going back to the home, then to the marae – over those three days, the end is the part that is the most beautiful yet often also the most hōhā.

After the body is put in the grave, everyone has to get back down to the marae and wait at the gate because there is a finishing ceremony that ties everything up. The family are called back on, just like they were called on at the start. There is karanga and everyone else gathers and walks on with immediate family. We go up to the front of the house and there will be lots of photos of the loved one. We have karakia, then the immediate family is invited to sit down and there is more kōrero, going over what has just happened.

Some of the talk will be about coming out of the state of grief. A family in mourning is said to be wearing the clothes of death and now is the time to symbolically take off those clothes and lead the family back, away from the lamenting and into the world of life and light.

A lot of people get hōhā about having to go back to the marae and go through the whole tangi thing – the kōrero, the mihi. It feels like it's taking forever. It can be annoying, especially if it is not someone you know well.

But when it is your own grief that is at the heart of things, you feel differently. You can just listen to the kōrero, have a laugh, have a cry, have a prayer, have a song. And at the end, all the people in the wharenui will come past and hongi the immediate family to welcome them back into the world of living and light.

And then we go in to the wharekai and eat to our hearts' and stomachs' content. There is a beginning, middle and end to the process.

Certainly, everyone will disperse at some point and the immediate family will be left on their own, and there will be times when the sadness revisits them and they miss their loved one very much. But there is an extra piece of tradition to deal with that – the unveiling of the headstone.

Usually a year or so after the tangi, everyone will come back to the urupā and join together for the unveiling. A year is also roughly the time it takes for the soil to settle completely over the casket. We come together not to chew over our grief yet again, but to acknowledge that a year has gone by and, although we haven't forgotten our loved one, we are no longer holding on to them but are getting on with our lives. This is something to celebrate.

I think our modern unveiling is a variation of the hahunga process, and suited to contemporary life. The hahunga was what we did in the old days in some areas, when bodies would be placed in caves or stored in a tree for the flesh to decay. Back then, our tūpuna wanted to end up with the bones of the dead person and nothing else. So they would put the body away, until everything had rotted away and all that was left were the bones. Then the bones would be buried and that was the final part of the process. The urupā was always marked, but not necessarily who was in it. Whereas before, we had the interring, disinterring, then reinterring, today we bury people only once.

But we have replaced the ancient practice with the unveiling, which combines the old Māori hahunga process with the contemporary European one of marking a grave with a headstone. It shows how Māori and Pākehā culture can influence each other.

A physical monument, such as the headstone, wasn't part of ancient tradition. But I am glad we adopted it. To me, it says that although we have buried the body and will not see that person again, we have provided something physical and permanent to remember them by.

For a husband and wife, it serves a purpose. It is a way of saying that enough time has passed for them to move on from the old relationship, so they can remarry. It also shows that they have completed their task and done everything they could for the dead person.

And providing a headstone means that when you go back to visit your loved one, there is something beautiful for you to contemplate, not just a mound of earth and a painted cross. A photo and some beautiful words will usually be part of the headstone and it's not unusual to see people kissing the photo.

Every religion has their own format for an unveiling, but usually there will be a karakia to open up, followed by a hīmene, then two people will lift up the veil covering the headstone. In a Catholic ritual, the priest will come with holy water and bless the grave.

But if you don't have a tradition for dealing with your sorrow, then you might want to go to a grief counsellor. We have names of counsellors on file but our clients don't ask for them. There have been times when I've thought it might be a good idea because people aren't dealing well with their loss, so I suggest it to them. But among Māori there is a strong feeling against counselling so they always turn me down.

GROWING UP, I learnt a lot about Māori funerals. When I finally got around to doing my funeral director training course, I got to learn a lot about Pākehā funerals. And I got to teach Pākehā a little about Māori ways.

For most of the people on the course, the ratio of Māori to Pākehā funerals was the opposite to mine. They were keen to hear about my customers and their expectations, and I was keen to hear about theirs.

Most had done at least a few Māori funerals but been left perplexed by some things. They couldn't understand the Māori attitude to time. Why did people say they wanted to get the body straight away, then not turn up after the funeral director had rushed to get it ready?

I had to explain that there would be a good reason as far as the family was concerned, such as that they were waiting for someone they really wanted to be present for the karakia – and, of course, they wanted the body to be ready for whenever that person did turn up.

But I was also able to provide some solutions. I explained how all the traditions fit together and why it was important for people to do all of them. When it was a case of 'We're waiting for Uncle to come and do the prayer,' it might be because Uncle was the only one who knew how. So if they – the Pākehā funeral directors – all learnt enough te reo Māori to do the karakia and could say it on behalf of everyone, then things could get moving.

Then there was the big topic that everyone was too shy to talk about – Māori also have a different attitude to time and its relationship to paying the bill. I knew this would be on their minds, so I made it easy for them by bringing it up first.

'You know my people are the worst,' I said. 'We are late to pay bills.'

Everyone was still being very polite, even after I'd said it: 'Well, possibly, now that you mention it ... I suppose I'd have to agree ... Perhaps sometimes I might have noticed that ...'

'Have you ever had difficulties getting payment from Māori families?' I asked.

Everyone put their hand up.

'We say, "Whānau, if you don't have the deposit, I can't help you,"' I said.

'Do you charge a deposit?' They couldn't believe it.

When a family has been grieving and showing their love for the one who has died, and they have done so with no food in their stomachs, eventually they run out of tears.

'Yes. You have to be straight up with your families. And if they don't provide the deposit, give them the number of another funeral director. And it's the same when it comes to doing things on time. If you want us to stay up and dress a body by two o'clock in the morning, you'd better have their clothes with us by four o'clock on the afternoon before. Otherwise you can wait till ten or eleven the next morning.'

'Do you speak to them like that?'

'You must. If you're too nice, they will push you over.'

This was the advice I had been given by employers in my early days as a funeral director. Thirty or forty years ago we had a generation that took their responsibilities seriously and collected the koha to pay for funerals. Today, people are finding it harder to pay. What I said may have sounded harsh but I hope my classmates went back to their firms in a more tolerant frame of mind because they understood more of the background of what was going on.

I also talked to them about how to make life easier for families. For instance, don't even show them expensive caskets, because once they see them they will want to get the best, because they think that is showing more respect for their loved ones.

If they show you their credit card, show them one kind of casket. If you've picked the body up from a home where you can see the people are struggling, show them another kind. That is what we do at Tipene Funerals.

Some families are great. They are honest and direct up front. They tell me what their limited budget is and I know what I have to deal with and can make it work. I can always find a way to help people somehow. The problems start when people want a $10,000 funeral on a $150 Work and Income cheque.

*

NINETY PER CENT of our business is Māori or Pasifika funerals – partly because people know I am part-Māori and part-Tongan, but mainly because those are the people we have developed the skills to serve. I would like more Pākehā funerals, of course. It would mean more business, but also there are things I like about Pākehā and the way they do funerals.

I like how organised Pākehā are. When I am doing an arrangement and we come to discuss the order of service and who will do the eulogy, they will already have decided who is going to speak for the family. Most times, they write down what they are going to say and have put a lot of thought into it. They speak from the mind. Māori speak from the heart. Despite our tradition of oratory, the person who stands up to kōrero is not always the most eloquent.

In some ways, Pākehā take things more slowly, and I've had to learn not to rush them. Māori want their loved ones prepared and back home as soon as possible. But Pākehā need to process the fact of death before they make any decisions. They often want me to wait a day before picking up the body – until they are sure what they want done with it.

I love how they trust us to do so many things, such as dressing their loved ones in the clothes they have chosen. At the same time, I enjoy suggesting that they do things differently, perhaps in a more Māori way.

'Would you like to watch to watch us dress Mum?'

'Can we do that?'

'Yes, you can.'

'Then yes, we'd love to.'

I only started encouraging this after learning about Pākehā funerals at the first firm I worked for.

'What time would you like to come and dress Mum?' I said, assuming they would.

'Oh no. Could you dress Mum?'

'Me?' Because with Māori, the funeral director didn't do the dressing. I had to adapt to this different way.

'What address should we take Mum home to?'

'Oh no, we're not taking her. She's going to stay here.'

Oh, really – all by herself? That's sad, I used to think, but never said out loud.

And that was how it was.

For Pākehā, when it came to the idea of dressing Mum, in their minds they thought they would have to go into a mortuary where she would be naked, lying on a steel table – but that's not how it is. It takes place in a dressing room. There is a nice towel or blanket covering Mum and all the dressing takes place under the blanket. It's something I learnt to do at Lagoon View and I think it's beautiful because it means the family can do something for Mum right at the very end of her time with them.

Also, Pākehā *love* being on time. Most people arrive at a Pākehā funeral within a few minutes of each other, not in dribs and drabs. That makes it a lot easier for me. If I get to the door with the service sheets half an hour before we are due to start, I can guarantee there will be some people already there because they wanted to make sure they would find a parking space.

Pākehā funeral arrangements are all about the day and the service and what will happen then, including the burial or cremation. And because it has all been so carefully planned, what you expect to happen will happen. There aren't many surprises at Pākehā funerals.

A Pākehā funeral has a very clear beginning, middle and end. A tangi definitely has a beginning, you might be able to work out when the middle has begun, and it will probably end at some stage, though it's not easy to predict when.

I'm not saying one kind of funeral is better than another, just pointing out that different cultures do things differently and I like both.

Pākehā and Māori have different attitudes to many things, and because Pākehā are more predictable, my job is easier. I charge the same for each kind of funeral, but the Māori one will have been a lot more work for me, partly because of the different things Māori need from a tangi, many of which go beyond the basics that Pākehā want.

The other day I was watching a funeral director from a well-known company finish up a funeral at Mangere Lawn Cemetery. I was a bit envious. I thought: *You've probably done half the hours of work I have for your fee. And you haven't had to be policeman, lawyer, judge and all the other roles I sometimes have to fill for Māori families.*

SO NOW I'VE TOLD YOU what I like about Pākehā funerals as opposed to Māori funerals, let me tell you why I love Māori funerals as opposed to Pākehā funerals.

For a start, I am directly connected to the tradition that supports Māori funerals. Luckily, because of my education in tikanga, I can fill in the gaps many families have in their traditional knowledge. It's become an important part of my job. I'm certainly no expert, but I work very hard to use my own limited knowledge to make sure they get the sort of funeral that does justice to their heritage.

A lot of urbanised Māori families haven't been brought up with the tikanga and the kawa of the marae, so when we arrive at a marae or home as part of the funeral, they will always look to me to lead and guide them.

I do the karakia and the whaikōrero to acknowledge everyone and the deceased, and a waiata, all in te reo Māori. I am very privileged to do that. I always get nervous when people ask me to. I always ask first if they have someone who is fluent and can kōrero. I don't want to muck it up. The dead family member is a person they know and I don't, and they're asking me to speak about this person to people who do know them. I try to generalise everything so I won't annoy anyone.

But I never say no. And it's not an invoiced item – it's just something I do.

I love the oratory that is part of a tangi. But it's much better if there are more experienced speakers than me on hand. When I listen to these people, I am in awe of their ability and I learn so much from what they have to say. My wife and I just stare at each other in amazement sometimes, especially if we take a funeral onto a marae. It is my university.

A lot of what I know about the differences between various cultures is what I have learnt doing their funerals.

When I first saw Samoans eating around the body, I thought, *What's going on here?* That went against my beliefs. Māori tradition is the complete opposite: there is no way you can have food near a body. Food is noa. You can't even take food into a church because the church space is tapu. For Samoans, it is completely different.

But food also has a part to play at a Māori funeral. After a tangi on a marae you will be invited in for kai and a cup of tea. Because food and drink are noa, eating and drinking takes the tapu off you.

At Indian funerals, I'm embarrassed to say, I always get hungry because I love curry and the smell is everywhere – from the funeral home, to the church, to the crematorium. It's so beautiful.

These experiences have been eye openers for me and I've had to use them to educate my staff. Once you understand what a person's religion or cultural beliefs are, then you can do a good job for them. You know what they will require at every step of the way.

And now cultures are mixing more and everyone's traditions are influencing everyone else's. Once, funeral homes held bodies in 'slumber rooms', where family could come to visit for half an hour or so before the funeral. Now we have rooms where family members can stay over with their relatives, and many do. We provide mattresses on the floor and people bring their own bedding. On the other hand, more and more Pākehā families are taking their relatives home where they can all be together for one last time. That's an example of tikanga influencing Pākehā culture. It's beautiful that both cultures are influencing each other to honour their dead.

He pōkēkē a Uenuku i tū ai

Dark clouds herald the appearance of a rainbow

CHAPTER FIFTEEN

AN UNVEILING
AND A REVELATION

AFTER MY COUSIN Luke, my beloved pop is the only other close relative I have lost. He died in January 2018. He had a very traditional tangi up at the marae with a requiem mass celebrated by his nephew Father Peter Tipene. It was held in the wharenui because the number of people was too big for the local church.

Pop's death hit me hard. My emotional reaction took me completely by surprise. He had been a father figure, there for me all my life, but after so much time spent helping other people with their experience of death, I found I was unprepared for the shock. Being in my position, you think you'd acquire so much knowledge and know what to do, but it's different when you experience it yourself.

Normally I breeze through all the paperwork and get the death notice done and dusted very quickly. But when it came to putting some words together for Pop – who was a very simple man – I was completely blank. It was the same as it had been with Luke.

I knew what going through the process meant – it meant accepting Pop was dead, and I obviously wasn't ready to do that. I struggled to find words and Kaiora had to help me all the way.

What normally would have taken me fifteen minutes took two hours. Finally, I gave it to Kaiora to check, my eyes full of tears.

'Do you think this is okay?' I asked her.

'Of course it is.'

'I just want to make sure.'

'It definitely is. It sounds so much like your pop. It's words from your heart.'

It was too. I was glad she could see that.

At Easter 2019, we had the long-planned unveiling of his headstone at Pawarenga. It didn't go quite the way I planned.

I would have had to prepare the unveiling whether I was the funeral director or not, because I have taken on – or been given – a lot of responsibility in Nan's family. I'm not the eldest grandchild, but I am the eldest grandson and everyone had looked to me for advice about what to do for Pop's tangihanga and after. I was supposed to have all the answers. Even when I couldn't give answers, because we hadn't discussed certain issues as a family, they seemed happy for me to make the decisions.

Just over a year after the tangi and it was time for the unveiling of Pop's headstone. We had spent a long time preparing for this. Nan wanted everything to be perfect and we didn't want to let her down. If she wanted it, it would happen. On the Thursday and Friday of Easter, we cleaned the cemetery, polished the grave, did some painting and found all the flowers we could to make everything beautiful.

There were three other family members having unveilings at

the urupā at the same time. The graves were all in a line stepped down a hill – one Tipene and three Wharewaka. They are my grandmother's brothers.

When we started planning, I thought we might get about 150 people. We got 250. Whānau were coming from all over. I was in shock. I thought with holiday traffic, people would decide it wasn't worth the hassle of coming all this way. I wouldn't have come. I would have sent my love and thoughts and been done with it. But people we hadn't seen in years came out of the woodwork.

It made a lot more work and also made it expensive.

Normally, my wife and I would stay on the marae, but with five children – including a four-month-old – it wasn't really practical for us to sleep in the wharenui with everyone else. You don't want to be the people whose baby's crying is waking everyone else up. So we took up our six-berth campervan and slept in that. We took another two campervans for people who were our guests, which meant that fifteen people were taken out of the accommodation equation, but resources would still be stretched.

The headstone itself was built like a miniature temple. It's made of black granite, with two pillars in front and a roof on top. Half the space was left for Nan, who will join Pop there when she dies.

It also has something we see on a lot of headstones in town now – digital memories on the headstone itself. There is a little porcelain QR square, and you can take a scanner and wave it around and everything about the person comes up on your device: photos, favourite music, whakapapa, where they lived, anything the whānau want remembered. It's like their own website attached to a headstone.

You can make them private or public. At Manukau Memorial Gardens, for instance, if you walk along the row and see someone you are interested in, you might be able to find out about them. That's a beautiful way for the new generation to find out more about their tūpuna.

I realised all this being done for Pop was a little bit over the top for someone who was a very simple man. I knew people would say, 'Oh, that's not him.'

'Yep, it's not him,' I was ready to tell them. 'But it's me, and I paid for it.' Also, it is my grandmother, and she is going in there too. She can be quite dramatic and over the top, so it's the way it is because it is for her as well as for him.

It was expensive, but I am happy with that. My wife and I had been trying hard to save to buy a home for our family. We still haven't had much luck so far, and extra expenses like a headstone don't help. But we discussed it and agreed that we wanted something special for Pop and Nan, so we would go all out and that would be the end of the big expenses. It would be better if we had won Lotto, but we hadn't. It was something we wanted to do and when it was over, we knew that we had done the best we could. Having honoured Pop, we could then think about ourselves and go back to saving for our home. I'm sure he will be grateful and bless us by helping us find a home at some point.

My grandfather's grave is different from the graves of his brothers-in-law. Theirs have been sealed permanently, but his couldn't be because we had to leave room for Nan. I insisted we have granite that could be opened up, which was a big expense. I felt for my family with this hōhā I created. It was all my fault. But the alternative would have been to leave it as a mound of dirt with the headstone at the end, and that wouldn't have looked right.

There was so much to be done for the unveiling, with so many people coming. The other big part of the job was cleaning up the cemetery. The family had been up every weekend for four weeks before Easter preparing the site. If you google 'St Gabriel's Church, Pawarenga', you will see in the picture they use that it has been a bit overgrown. So, we needed to do a lot of mowing, weed-eating, spraying and water-blasting. Also, we cleaned other headstones and repainted words that had come off after many years.

We paid for it a little differently from the way we used to do things in my childhood. The traditional way was to rely on koha to pay for everything. This time, we had a family fundraising effort to cover expenses.

There were a few more expenses than usual too. I asked that we have the main day catered so that as a family we could all be part of the ceremony. The traditional way of doing things splits families up. Half of them can attend the ceremony and really be part of things. The other half are stuck back in the kitchen, peeling potatoes and taking care of the roast.

So we got in caterers, who also happened to be part of our extended family. I wanted something special, so it wasn't an ordinary hangi but a buffet with beautiful platters of all sorts of food. Pastry puffs and pineapple pies instead of steamed pudding. It was food like we see at funerals in Auckland.

In the days and weeks before, Nan kept thinking of extra things I needed to do.

'Francis, I need tablecloths.'

'Sure thing, Nan. How many? Four?'

'No, I think we need forty.'

My colleague Stan was in charge of lights. He lit the dining room so it had a nice colour. The wharekai wasn't big enough to hold everyone at mealtimes, so I had to take up the company gazebo to feed the children in. We got 160 chairs up from Tauranga and they will stay at the marae to be used in the future. We also took up twelve tables for the buffet.

No matter how hard you try to organise everything, there will always be something unexpected to trip you up. I've learnt not to expect too much because you can easily get disappointed. In your mind, you see how it's going to run, but it may not turn out like that. Especially when you are not in the city. We don't have a lot of resources in Pawarenga and it is an hour's drive to Kaitaia. But we also are not stuck in rigid time frames. We are at home. We don't need to hurry up and get out because the next funeral is waiting outside.

I also had to get a grip on my perfectionism. Any little thing that is out of place annoys me to the point where until it's fixed I can't relax. But I know that most people, as long as they feel welcome and have a good kai, will not worry or complain. They will sense that it is done well and not get hung up on the details, like I do.

There were a lot of family dynamics involved in the preparation. One of my uncles had two families from two wives and we had to make arrangements to deal with that. Another uncle had children in the South Island, which complicated things. Another had children who were estranged, so we had to find them. We had managed to get all those things sorted in the lead-up to the weekend.

You don't normally have order of service sheets – the printed prayers and pictures for people to follow – for an unveiling. But I thought it would be a nice touch that would help make the occasion even more special. I got some prepared showing the sequence of events, the hymns we would sing, the words of the blessings and the names of people who would be doing readings and who would actually officiate and do the unveiling of the headstones. I got photos of my grandfather and uncles and put one on each page.

I wanted people to have a nice piece of memorabilia to take home and keep as a souvenir. The older generation love the order of service sheets they get at funerals. I know many of them keep them all together as a record of the loved ones they have lost. I have had people tell me they still have the sheets from the very first funerals I did in the early 2000s. It was another expense for the unveiling, but I felt it was worth it.

That was a mistake, as I'll explain.

On the first day, not only did everyone who had RSVPed turn up, so did a whole lot more people. We had to do an awful lot of pōwhiri. We had arranged access to two wharenui for everyone to sleep in but even they weren't going to be enough, so we had to rent another marae up the road.

Everyone turned up on Friday and they were clearly going to stay until Monday. If it had been me, I would have just driven up for the day. I couldn't help wondering how long it would take those who left on Monday to get home in the horrendous Easter traffic.

But I was in a shock of love. I couldn't believe all these people came to pay their respects and celebrate with us when they could have been doing other things. This was the first sign that I was a bit out of touch with my own culture. I felt greatly grounded by looking around at the whānau. I'm so lost. I'm such an Aucklander. I would not be sleeping on a marae. But these people came for the kaupapa with open hearts, ready to work and contribute.

There was an extra dimension to the weekend because we also had a burial. A stillborn baby girl who one of my Wharewaka cousins had lost was brought up from Christchurch to be put to rest on our marae.

So we had a little tangihanga. The baby came on and was placed in the wharenui – like a normal tangi. We had a pōwhiri, a karanga, karakia, mihimihi and afterwards a little haka. Then we took the baby from the marae up to the urupā.

Originally, the cousin wanted to bring the baby straight to the cemetery, but I was told by a kaumātua that a stillborn baby is more sacred and more tapu than an adult. It was important that the baby come to the marae first so we could pay our respects to her and then she would be interred on top of her grandfather.

That grave had to have the concrete poured after the baby was interred. We had just enough time for it to dry so it would be ready for everything on Sunday. There couldn't have been a better reason to hold things up a bit than doing justice to this mokopuna. It's very special that she and her grandfather are now together.

I LEARNT a couple of good lessons that weekend.

The preparation wasn't completed until the early hours of Sunday morning, the day of the unveiling itself. It was a beautiful Northland day and everything was perfect at last.

Well, nearly everything. Not far from Pop's grave was a patch of untidy grass with cabbage trees and, to me, it disturbed the look of the beautifully mown cemetery. I wanted to get in there and weed eat and clear it out, but my uncles told us not to because some important person's bones were buried there and it was very tapu.

I argued, 'Okay, yes there are bones and bodies buried there in unmarked graves. I get that. But why can we not clean it up – with respect and love – to represent them and to give us space to acknowledge these kaumātua and tohunga?'

'If you want to mess around there,' said my uncle, 'you should know people have gone down there – and their kids have died.'

Don't give me that crap, I thought. *I respect what is tapu. I'm not coming in as a smart arse, knowing better. But why are these things never talked about? At least give us some reasons.* All I wanted was an explanation as to why we couldn't honour our loved ones and give them the respect they deserve by tidying things up. It wasn't a big space, just a bit of overgrown lawn. The whole cemetery looked tidy and beautiful except this bit.

To my mind, our tūpuna were there and we should do everything we could to show our respect, not leave them lying under overgrown scrub and cabbage trees.

I wanted wānanga and kōrero with my uncles and aunties. I wanted to know why we had to keep scaring generation after generation by saying children will die or someone will be taken from you.

Some people would say I shouldn't have got so upset over a patch of long grass: 'Francis, this is your OCD at work.' Maybe it was. But there was also a bit of the cemetery that was just hideous.

Not everyone agreed with me. My cousins said being on TV had gone to my head.

'Maybe so,' I said, 'but I still want to know why we do what we do. Just tell me a logical reason as to why we shouldn't respect and tidy up the grave and I will be content. Do you think it's good enough to just say it's tapu and one of my kids will die if I touch it?'

'That's right.'

'So for the rest of our lives we're going to leave this bit of patchy grass here?'

All of our lives we do things because our tūpuna did, and I always ask why, and no one can ever tell me. No one else asks. And the only answer I ever get is: 'Because Uncle said and that's the law.' But I want to know why that's the law. We don't have a lot of written records of why things are the way they are, so I need a person to tell me.

I had heard the stories about not going in there when I was younger, and I knew there were tūpuna there. Now that I've grown up and am a bit more aware of the world and tapu and sacredness, I still don't understand why we can't mow it.

Anyway, it stayed unmown for the unveiling – I didn't want my children to die. I lost that battle and everything went ahead with that ugly-as piece of grass just sitting there.

THAT'S ONE CONFLICT. But there was another one that was very sad and a lesson for me. On the Saturday night before the ceremony, there was a hui. The bell rang and the whole 250 people sat there for evening karakia. I was swept away by how beautiful it was to hear everyone singing.

When the religious part was finished, it was time for some kōrero. My cousin Aterea, who is a kaumātua, got up and started speaking. It was all in te reo Māori.

'Kia ora, whānau,' he said, 'we're all here now and we have the unveiling tomorrow so we need to talk and discuss like we did in the old days who is going to unveil and who is going to read each headstone.'

Oops, I thought to myself. *Hi, everyone, I'm here.* So I stood up and spoke.

'I want to let everyone know we've decided who is reading and who is unveiling,' I said. 'I've already made up order of service sheets and I've got one here for you to look at.' And I had a few to hand around and show people.

'Okay … And who did you run this by?' said my cousin.

When I was preparing it, I had given it to my grandmother and her sister. Their job was to ring around the family to ask who would do the reading and who would do the unveiling.

'The right thing to do is the night before the unveiling we talk about it and we ask who is here,' said Aterea. 'We might have a VIP or a kaumātua who has turned up unexpectedly who we want to give that honour to. We might want Aunty to read it – not necessarily you, Francis.'

I was going to do my Pop's reading.

It was awful, I felt so bad. I had a lot of whakamā.

'I am deeply sorry for going over people's heads,' I said. 'It was just what I thought would be nice to do, and it would be nice for everyone to have something to take away.'

'Oh well, now you've learnt your lesson. This is how we do things.'

I was surprised how many of my younger cousins knew that was the process. I thought because all our uncles who were the leaders were dead that we would be able to do things slightly differently, while still respecting tradition. But it was my cousins and others of my age group who wanted to hold on to my uncles' values.

So I acknowledged that and apologised to 250 people and thought that would be the end of my embarrassment, but it wasn't. Some of the people who had been named to do readings or unveilings popped up and said they didn't know anything about it. They asked who I got the information from.

'Excuse me,' I said. 'I got this from my grandmother and my aunty. They called you all personally and you said that it is how you're going to do it.'

I forced myself to stay calm in the middle of this kōrero. I knew that once I said something I wouldn't be able to take it back. So I didn't say what I wanted to say, which was: 'If you all don't shut up right now I will take the gazebo away, along with all the food I bought. You have come here and you are going on to me about tikanga. Real tikanga is about how you feed the people, and I bet tomorrow you will all be happy to have your stomachs full.' It would have been really cheeky, but it is how I felt.

But it turned into one of those arguments. I shouldn't have been surprised. We're not very good at agreeing with each other up north.

But I learnt that if I have to do something like this again, I will need to consult more widely. I thought there had been proper consultation. I thought I had done the right thing by talking to my nan, who is the oldest, and the others.

Ultimately, things happened pretty much according to the order of service I had prepared anyway, with just a couple of names changed. But it only happened like that because the others wanted it to.

*

STILL, THERE WAS A LOT to enjoy about the weekend. There were a lot of people there we hadn't met before. And there was the satisfaction of people working together. People were divided into three groups: one for cleaning the marae, one for preparing food, one for doing dishes. It gave us the opportunity to meet and mingle and work out who everyone was. It was like a family reunion being held alongside the unveiling. I made connections and established relationships with cousins I never knew I had.

Many of these cousins were not the result of long-term relationships, if I can put it that way. But they are still part of the whānau, of course. Explaining the connections could be quite complicated and funny.

'I'm the sister between this brother and this brother.'

'But Uncle was married to their mother when both of them were born. That doesn't make sense. How did you get in the middle? … Ohhhh.'

That is life.

TV reared its head too – a lot of people mentioned *The Casketeers*, especially the new cousins.

'We know you but you don't know us.'

'That's neat,' I said. 'Tell me who you are.'

Kaiora and I didn't need to be introduced because *The Casketeers* had broken the ice. We could just start having kōrero with these people and pretty soon we were connecting like any other whānau on a grassroots level.

And I especially loved seeing my children getting to know and bond with cousins they had never met.

One of my aunties brought a horse down with a bridle and saddle and left it there for the weekend. It was a huge hit. All day, the kids were riding it or walking with it or taking photos with it. It was so good to see my kids off their iPads. There's no coverage in Pawarenga anyway. Of course, iPads have their good and bad points. I just don't like seeing them on them all the time.

The marae is right next to the beach. In fact, you have to drive on the beach to get to it, so there is only access at low tide. It's a harbour so it's very calm, with no waves. In fact, it's quite boring as oceans go. But that means it's safe for kids and they made the most of it too. They were able to have fun in the middle of everything else – it was all part of the weekend.

They had the water, the horse, the creek and there was always an abundance of food, so it was also a beautiful holiday at the same time as re-energising, re-invigorating and getting to meet more of their extended whānau.

And it also meant my wife and I could get a little bit of time in the middle of all the busy-ness to talk to each other face to face instead of by text or phone, which doesn't often happen in the chaos of Auckland and Tipene Funerals.

I was reminded of that when we got back into phone range and there was a mountain of messages from my staff. They had had our busiest weekend ever. I told them if that happened again they should advise people to go to other funeral homes. We often do that, but just as often people say no that's fine, they are happy to wait until we can fit them in.

ONCE I GOT HOME I couldn't let the fuss over the piece of grass go. I did know a little bit of the background about the urupā. Long

'We need to get a shovel
and bang the ground.
If it sounds hollow,
there is no one there.'

ago, some bones that had been stored up on the hill got washed down into the valley when there were some big floods.

Those bones were placed in unmarked graves – where the messy grass is – and in among them are the bones of an important chief. He was a powerful figure when he was alive and although the remains have been there for ages, and are certainly a long way down by now, the elders don't want us to mess with anything.

That left me still with a lot of questions.

As it happened, not long after the unveiling for Pop's and my uncles' headstones, I had to go to Pawarenga for another tangi. My lovely Aunty Chrissie, Nan's sister, had a fall at home and died.

While I was there, I caught up with my uncle Nick Adams or Mataki Adams, who is named after my great-grandfather. He's the family rangatira and he makes all the important calls.

I was always scared of him when I was growing up because he was the growly one who laid out the harsh realities. My view was that he wasn't open to the way the real world is. My attitude had been that there was no point asking him anything because he would just say no.

But he sought me out and we had a good kōrero. When someone tells me something that is connected to my world I take it all in. He has shared a lot.

It all started with the arrangements being made for Aunty Chrissie's tangi. The correct kawa in a case like this is to sort out the details – like where someone will be buried and when you will get the body to the marae – so everyone can have some input.

'It's time to sit down and talk about things,' said my uncle.

There are two cemeteries at Pawarenga – the old one at St Gabriel's, where my grandfather is, and a new whānau cemetery – so the first thing was to decide which one my aunty would be buried in. Everyone knew Nan really wanted her sister to be buried in the old one but it is full to capacity.

'What would the family like to do?' said Uncle Nick. 'What time would they like the tangi and where?'

I had been asked to act as spokesperson for the family.

'Uncle, the family have requested that Aunty be buried at the old urupā up here on Thursday at ten o'clock.'

This was what we wanted, even though we knew we wouldn't get it. The cemetery was full to capacity and the normal time for funerals up north is 11 am.

'Okay,' said Uncle. 'We'll see what we can do. We'll go up, probe the ground and hopefully there will be a space there for Aunty.'

I was gobsmacked. I had just thought I'd throw it out there. I never dreamt we would get it. I knew Aunty had to go to the new cemetery. We all thought my grandfather was going to be the last one in the old cemetery.

Then another kaumātua got up: 'I'm sorry, everyone, but up here in the north we always have our tangi at eleven o'clock, so that latecomers have time to get here and make their farewells.'

'If you want to have it at ten, that makes sense because the new generation has to get back to Auckland,' said Uncle. 'They have jobs to go to. If we want to keep the younger generation involved, we have to adapt and meet them halfway.'

Honestly. Where was this coming from? It was true, of course. We did need to go back. But everyone was flabbergasted.

It was a profound moment for me, because I suddenly had a new appreciation for Uncle and the way he thought. It meant we had evolved. We had integrated our new ways of life into the old ways and they all worked together. It was a beautiful moment.

'The first thing we have to do is go up to the cemetery and see if we can find a plot,' he said.

So Uncle and I went up to the cemetery and on the way he started giving me information. It was a little bit scary. I felt like he was imparting knowledge because he needed to – almost as though it was important to do this now in case he died.

It is part of his responsibility to pass on the knowledge he has to someone else. But he wasn't the type to sit down and record things or let someone write them down. He was working in the old tradition for transmitting wisdom – all done orally from one person to another. I wished there had been someone else there to witness it and help me take it all in.

But, I thought, since he was in this frame of mind, I would take the opportunity to ask some questions that I'd had for a long time.

Now was my chance to clear up a few things – especially that patch of grass. Uncle filled in some of the gaps for me. It turns out there was once an old tohunga who was one of our tūpuna and not a nice man. Uncle didn't go into detail about why he wasn't nice, but I was happy to take his word for it. And he is the important person whose bones have been put in the unmarked patch.

'Every time someone goes in there,' said my uncle, 'he will say, "Get out and leave us alone. Let us rest in peace."'

Before, I just didn't believe in any of that stuff at all, but hearing our kaumātua tell it to me person to person was different. I kept asking questions.

'Really? But why couldn't we clean that area up anyway? He's been dead for a long time.'

'You will know when the time is right to go and clear that up.'

'Uncle, I was here a month ago and the time was right.'

But maybe it wasn't. I know more now. Those bones that got washed down out of the cave area are still tapu. I didn't want to be put off clearing this wāhi tapu by scary stories designed to frighten children. But I also wanted to respect other people's beliefs and that was easier to do if I knew the whole story. Uncle has helped me see this. And I believe I will know when the time is right to mow that grass.

But the main issue we still had to deal with was that we needed to find somewhere to bury Aunty. The urupā was full. There is a fence we could have moved but unfortunately that would take us on to land that belongs to another family.

Graves are all around the church and a walkway runs alongside them. But at the top of the row of graves was a little bare spot. Uncle and I walked up there.

'There is a space here,' he said. 'We need to get a shovel and bang the ground. If it sounds hollow, there is no one there. If it doesn't, or if you don't hear an echo, there is someone there.'

I thought he was pulling my leg. But he said he knew there was an available space right here in the urupā. However, we still had to check because over the years things had changed so much that there might be body bits all over the place.

After that kōrero, I snuck off to get a shovel and went back to try it by myself. First, I banged it on the patch of ground where he said no one was. I did it so hard that the shovel bounced back and nearly hit me in the face. I only just got out of the way in time. So there was definitely no hole there.

Then I went to where he said there are graves that are unmarked, and I hit my shovel on the ground and it didn't bounce. So I went back and tried again. Banged the first one, it bounced; banged the second one, it didn't bounce.

I was still having trouble believing he knew this. I even tried it with a different shovel to be sure, but I got the same result.

I learnt a bit about tikanga from Uncle Nick. And I also learnt that I had been a bit big-headed. I didn't know everything after all. I needed to stop trying to justify everything and find an answer to everything. I should rely a bit more on kōrero and spirituality to get me though life.

I could probably get a scientist to come up to Pawarenga and run some tests and conclude that because the gradient is this way here and the water table is this way there then this happens and that happens. But I don't need to do that, because I've got Uncle.

Over the next little while, we got into some more conversation. There was so much I wanted to know about what things had been like in the old days.

'What was it like when they had tangi here when you were young?' I asked him.

'Things were different back then,' he told me. At least, they were for him. When there was a tangi, the kids had to do all the normal things to help, like working in the kitchen and preparing kai. After that, most of the kids were allowed to go out and play but Uncle had been chosen to learn the traditions. He had to go and sit in the wharenui and listen to the kōrero that went on there – absorb and learn. That's why he has so much respect from so many people in the north. Because he is the one who took in all the knowledge. It's so beautiful he shared some with me.

'What did we bury the mate in before we had caskets?' I asked, and he told me about the first casket that was ever made in Pawarenga. It was just a plain piece of wood that the whānau built together. They thought the casket was very flash. But just after they built the first one, the great influenza epidemic hit and so many people died they couldn't keep up. They even ran out of tarpaulin.

When it came to preservation, Uncle told me it was done 'up at the Ghost Bridge'. I had heard about this but never knew why it had that name. As a child, I thought it was just because it was a dark spot deep in a valley.

Uncle explained that the people used to take the body up to the bridge. They washed it first by submerging it in the river. Then they rubbed kōkōwai on it. After that process, the body was taken back to the marae and left lying on a flax mat, unwrapped, until the final day of the tangi when it was put in the ground.

It was great to learn what our own personal traditions are. Hearing Uncle talk about the preparation of bodies and the rites that followed, and knowing that this was done to my tūpuna and people I knew, made it very special.

It also got me thinking it would be great to try and replicate it today. Although, I don't know what health and safety experts would say about preparing a body in a river, especially when they used to do it upstream rather than at the downstream end.

I felt so privileged and grateful to be receiving the gift of this knowledge. Everything else about the tangi then was the same as the tangi now: the kōrero, bringing the body on, karanga, whaikōrero. Only now we have electric lights.

After this kōrero and transmission of knowledge had taken place, we had my aunty's tangi. But Uncle Nick hadn't finished with organising graves for people. At one stage, he asked for me and I answered the summons. He was standing near Aunty's grave site.

'Right here is another place we can put someone,' he said.

'Okay,' I said, thinking, *Can I get someone else to witness this*, because it was a lot to take in.

'Right there and right there,' said Uncle Nick. 'Two people can fit here, or four if they go on top of each other.'

I got my cousin Ted to come and listen to this imparting of information so I would have someone to back me up down the track. Otherwise there would be a tangi in a couple of years where I would end up fighting with other kaumātua.

We also talked a little on that visit about another kind of death – not of people but of culture and tikanga. How can these be kept alive? Of course, nearly all children learn some of it at school these days – or have the opportunity to. As a family, up north we have two or three males who can kōrero in fluent reo. But when we get up there for any big gathering, everyone runs for the kitchen and leaves front of house to us few. That's the talking and decision-making left to us and the others don't take an opportunity to learn. I worry about the future for our valley and our culture.

Ko tō manawa, e Kura,
ko tōku manawa, ka irihia

———————————

May your heart, oh Kura,
be bound and suspended with mine

CHAPTER SIXTEEN

WHĀNAU FIRST

I SAY 'I' in this book a lot. I really should say 'we' because there isn't much I do without Kaiora, and there's almost nothing I could do without her support. And she'd totally agree with that. She calls me her sixth son. 'I have five kids of my own but six including the husband,' she says. It's true. Sometimes I get a bit envious when I have to share her with the other boys and I come last.

At work, she is wonderful to talk things over with, and it's a shame that all her other commitments mean she can't do so many funerals because she is a wonderful funeral director too. But with keeping the business and family running and not coming apart at the seams she just doesn't have the time.

And I do plenty of things she finds irritating. Someone told her they thought I was easily distracted. She didn't totally agree. 'That depends,' she said. 'If someone throws a piece of banana bread in front of him ...'

Also, I struggle with budgets, especially if I see a bargain. Or a power tool I don't have. I know I'm not much of a handyman but I have a minor power tool addiction. I love them. I have an electric tool of every kind.

When I first put the leaf blower on my back, I felt empowered and like a real man for my wife. I thought I could build anything my wife wanted.

I can't do much building at the moment because we don't have our own house. I really need somewhere with a garage. I could try things out in the back of the funeral home, but you just get started on something and then a family comes to see their loved one so I can't make any noise. I've been practising on the decks of the hearses with a little cut-out Makita jigsaw and my safety glasses and earmuffs on.

And Kaiora doesn't really want me to build anything anyway. Apparently, it is more trouble than it's worth because the things I make might look good at first but fall apart quickly. She'd like me to pay someone to do those things but I want to do them myself. I'm like my grandfather in that respect. Except he could do it.

However, even Kaiora will tell you I can be romantic when necessary. And it is often necessary, especially after one of my budget blowouts or DIY-gone-wrong adventures. I'll let her tell the stories.

THE LATE FRANCIS TIPENE

Kaiora: I was working at our local MP Peeni Henare's office in Onehunga, doing electoral admin work, for a couple of years before *The Casketeers* started, fitting funeral work around it. One morning I had got really disappointed in Francis and I couldn't focus on my work. I didn't have to be in the office that day but I went because I didn't want to be at home having to look at him. It was pretty bad.

Then, completely unexpectedly, he came in with this boom box playing 'Can We Talk' at full volume. There were also red roses and chocolate hearts spelling out 'I love you'.

'There's no one here,' I said. 'Why haven't you done this when everyone's here to see it?'

So he took some photos and shared them on Facebook. I thought that was cute.

The other moment that really touched me was on a marae. He was doing his mihi and I was half listening because I already knew what was in it, then out of nowhere I heard my name and he was telling everyone how much he loves me and how beautiful I am. It was a really romantic buzz. I do feel appreciative when he acknowledges me and especially in those moments when it's unexpected.

On the other hand – he is really bad with dates. Last year on our anniversary, I said, 'Shall we go out for breakfast?'

'No, I've got work to do.'

He wasn't getting my hint.

'Would you like to go to lunch then?'

'What do you think I am – do you think this is just a play business?' he said.

'Well, happy anniversary to you too,' I snapped and walked out and slammed the door.

He felt so bad. After a couple of hours of me not speaking to him, he worked up the courage to come and find me.

'Have you seen my Facebook post?'

'No.'

'Well, you should.'

'Are you trying to apologise to me?'

'Look, I am sorry. I'm so sorry, but if you just read what I said you'll get what I mean.'

And he had written saying happy anniversary and thanks for tolerating me.

He's also really bad at surprises, but it's quite hard to surprise me when I'm the one monitoring all the credit card bills.

Having such a big family has been a surprise. We had the first two and we thought that would be it. Nikora arrived in 2005, Moronai in 2007. Then there was a five-year gap before I thought I was pregnant again. I told Francis.

'Are you sure?' he said. We were both in a bit of shock. So I took another test and I was and Mikae came in 2013.

Francis nearly missed that one. It was when we were at Waitakere Funerals and working hard. My mum had been nearby because she was always around when I was pregnant and the baby wasn't too far away. But she was away that night and there was no one else around.

By now, we well knew that I wasn't allowed to give birth except by Caesarean section. But at this time, I wasn't due for five weeks. I was also studying to be a teacher and had left work early to get things sorted. I had a lot on.

Then my waters broke. I really hoped it was something else, but then I saw a little show of blood. I should have rung the midwife. Instead, I rang Francis at work.

'I think my waters have broken.'

'What? They can't have.'

'I think they have, because now I'm bleeding.'

'No, no, no. You're not having a baby now.'

'Excuse me?'

'I'm about to start a service. I have to do a karakia.'

'I don't care what you have to do. I'm having a baby.'

'Could you just ring the midwife or ring your sister?'

I wasn't very happy. I rang the midwife and she told me to pack my bags and get to hospital and she would meet me there. I had my other two kids with me. Mum wasn't there. His sisters were out of town. Mine was in Hamilton. And I was having contractions.

I rang Francis back.

'This is too much,' he said. 'I'm about to have a karakia. Take the boys to the hospital and I'll get someone to meet them there.'

'No, you won't. You are coming to the hospital.'

I rang my best friend and she met me at the hospital and took over the kids till Francis got there. *If* he got there. I'm not sure what happened but the next thing I knew I was in theatre. Everything was ready to go for the Caesarean.

'Is your husband coming?' asked the doctor. 'We're going to theatre in fifteen minutes.'

'I don't know if he's coming or not, but if he's not here I'll go in without him.'

'Are you sure?'

'Yes. I'm doing it.'

'Okay.'

Then Francis rang.

'The doctor is here and I'm ready to go,' I told him. 'I can't stop these contractions.'

'Could you ask him to wait till midnight?'

'That's just rude.'

It turned out he wanted to finish work and tidy up the funeral home before coming to the birth. Also, before midnight was the same day as his cousin's son's birthday, and he didn't want that.

'If there's going to be any divorce in this relationship, it will be because of work,' I said.

'I just need to ask him —'

I put him on speaker.

'Yes, it's the doctor here.'

'This is Francis, Kaiora's husband. I was just wondering if you could wait until midnight.'

'This is a life-threatening situation for your wife and you're asking me to hold off until midnight?'

'Oh – that sounds really bad,' said Francis. 'Okay, I'm sorry, I'll do my best to get there.'

I was so disappointed in him.

I don't know where he was coming from, or what he had to do to get to the hospital on time, but he made it. I could hear his voice outside.

'Is that my husband?' I said.

'Yes, he is here and he is going to scrub up.'

But I was prepared to have a baby without him.

WHEN KAIORA GAVE BIRTH to Mikae, it had a very surprising effect. We didn't see it coming, but that baby brought a lot of joy to a lot of people. He was special because we had had the big gap between babies. In fact, we thought our baby days were over. No more bottles and nappies. The others were at school and we were deep into our careers.

Then this chubby, cute baby came along. He was so big he could hardly hold his head up and he didn't crawl till he was twelve months old or walk until he was fourteen months. And everyone adored him.

In any family with a lot of children, you evolve traditions. Just as we have iwi traditions, marae traditions and even Tipene Funerals traditions, we also have traditions within our whānau at home.

We have karakia together at night and in the morning before school to start our day. On Monday nights, we have family home evening when we get together to have a prayer, go round the room to discuss family events – what's coming up for everyone, any dramas at school or dramas at home – before we finish with another karakia.

The grandmothers have been part of our Monday night several times. A lot of Catholic prayers are repetitive but the Mormon tradition is to pray from the heart. And when the whaea hear their mokopuna saying, 'We thank thee for our grandmothers being here and staying the night,' they love it. They think it's beautiful and so do I.

It's good to have a quiet moment like that because domestic life does get a bit chaotic at times. At the pace we live, something has to give and, rather than that being us and our relationship or our parenting, we have outsourced some basic domestic responsibilities. We have a cleaner who cleans our home, we have a person who takes our washing away and brings it back, and Uber Eats has saved our lives. Every other night we have meals

Looking after your family and making sure you enjoy life is like doing exercise or eating well – it is something you have to prioritise or plan for because otherwise it is easy to let it slip.

delivered. Other nights my children love noodles and mince, or some nights if we're really lazy we'll heat up sausage rolls. But mince and mashed potato is the go-to in our home.

The outside assistance isn't just help with our home life, it's actually help with the business because it means Kaiora can play her part there, which is really important. The business would be so much less without her.

The boys are all finding their own interests. Moronai loves to go fishing with my father. He is the sporty one and plays league. Mikae takes after me and isn't at all sporty.

Not long ago we discovered cycling as something we could all enjoy doing together. It just came up one day when life and work and everything else were getting on top of us. Kaiora and I went to a bike shop and bought bikes for everyone, with trainer wheels or a trailer for the smallest ones.

And then we hit the road and cycled along Tamaki Drive to Mission Bay. We packed up some kai and a folding table and chairs and had a picnic. It was one of the best things we've ever done. And it wasn't something we had to try hard at. It wasn't about being the best bike rider, or the best bike rider who was also a funeral director, it was about having fun as a family.

When I had a chance to think about it, I realised we had let work take over. We were caught up in being a young couple trying to make sure we didn't fail. Life was work, work, work. We had been living in a funeral home for three years. The kids were put in their place and made to keep quiet. All they ever saw was us working.

And the solution was as simple as just riding a darn bike. It's a regular part of our lives now as soon as the weather gets warm.

It's important that the kids have things to look forward to – it's also a good way to keep them in line if there is a picture on the wall of something big that we are all looking forward to doing. And it helps them to understand us. They know Mum and Dad are doing all this work so we can do the big family things together.

There is always a cake and a dinner out when a birthday comes around. It used to be Wendy's but now it's somewhere a bit nicer. Also, I probably need to be kept away from Wendy's as much as possible. And on birthday mornings we sing 'Happy Birthday' when we have karakia.

When Kaiora and I were young, we could never take such things for granted. Kaiora's brother is in his mid-thirties and still talks about how on his ninth birthday, nothing happened. I don't know if everyone forgot or there was some other reason, but he is still sad that no one even sang 'Happy Birthday' for him then.

And Kaiora's dad was very tough about Christmas. The presents used to build up under the tree in the days and weeks before 25 December and on the day all these other things had to be done before they could open their presents. They had to have karakia, then hīmene, then a big lecture about the day and Jesus Christ their Saviour. And then they were finally allowed to open their presents.

That wouldn't work with our kids.

We also have a goal of a family holiday somewhere like Fiji or the Gold Coast every year. We'll stick to that goal. Looking after your family and making sure you enjoy life is like doing exercise or eating well – it is something you have to prioritise or plan for because otherwise it is easy to let it slip.

*

IN THE PAST few years, my father and his wife, Debbie, have become a much bigger part of our lives. That's brought more love into our family – and his sense of humour. That funny side of me people see on TV is actually from my father. He is always cracking people up.

I know there is such a thing as a Māori sense of humour, and there is probably a Tongan one as well. They work on the same level.

Sometimes, it's a bit outrageous.

One day my dad said to Mihaka, when my son was about four, 'Hey, you're an arsehole!'

'You're an arsehole,' said Mihaka back. And Kaiora and I were looking at each other wondering if we had just heard what we thought we had heard. And they went on calling each other arsehole for quite a while.

It was only funny because they have such a strong bond. In the proper world, no child would call his grandfather an arsehole, but this is our family, not the proper world. And it just cracked everyone up.

It's the grandchildren who have brought us all closer together. Kaiora and I bought a caravan a few years ago and started to go on holidays in it. Once, my dad and Debbie came along with their tent. The rain came and they started to get cold. We felt awful and asked them to come in but they wouldn't.

In the end, after much discussion and showing them the benefits of the caravan, they bought one too. And now we all go out so often, it's awesome. There's no TV, no nothing. We cook together, eat together and laugh all the time.

We camp around Coromandel a lot. If it's cold or raining, it doesn't matter because you're in the caravan. Caravans and pushbikes have brought us close together as a family. With five kids, holidays can be complicated and expensive. But not with a caravan.

The kids have found it a bit confusing that my surname is Tipene, from their grandmother's side of the family, and not Muller after their grandfather. When Francis Jr was born on my birthday at the end of 2018, my wife wanted to name him Francis Anthony, which is my name, and I thought maybe we should take it a little bit further.

'Why don't we honour my father and call him Francis Anthony Muller?' I said.

She thought it was a good idea and I really wanted to do it. But when we thought it through, we worried that it wouldn't make sense with the other kids. I was scared they would always wonder why one of them had a different name from the others. The intention was to honour my dad and our Tongan heritage. But the more important thing is that the kids love their grandfather and they know they have Muller in them.

IN OUR WIDER Tipene whānau, we have a tradition of family meetings every three months or so. It goes back to when our great-grandparents set up a committee to take care of basic funeral costs, which was a very far-sighted thing to do. They realised the sooner you start to plan for a funeral the better, and they wanted everyone to have a decent tangi without having to worry about how to pay for it.

It has been set up so that when family members turn eighteen and get a job, they start paying fees into an account. When there is a death in the family, that fund is there and used to cover essential expenses: kai, the funeral home, venues and other costs that have to be met for a funeral. There are various levels – couple fees, family fees and so on.

And we have the meetings to keep everything transparent, to talk about the account and how it's doing. Although there is a lot of general business discussed, it is ultimately about making sure the fund is being run properly. We have a constitution that forbids that money to be spent on anything other than funerals.

The hui never last more than a day. We check the bank account and have a mini-audit. If there has been a tangi since the last meeting, there will be an accounting of what was spent. Once that is over, we move on to the other issues – children, whānau, travelling, marriages, babies. We talk about anything and everything.

So it is about overall wellbeing. We get to catch up with other whānau members and see how everyone is doing, not just financially but in all respects. It means we can give help or advice to anyone who might need it. It keeps us connected and together.

The meetings were part of the fund right from when it was established. I grew up with them. All my great-grandparents' children – my grandparents and their siblings – take turns hosting them. We had one at Pawarenga at the time of Pop's unveiling because everyone was there anyway.

Even though the focus is on death, there is so much life in the meetings.

The young ones love it. In the past ten to fifteen years, there's been a move to get them more involved in activities, learning about their culture. We can let the schools take care of it or we can take care of it as a family. I prefer us to do it. It's beautiful involving the kids with the meetings, sharing in games and kai and with waiata to finish.

This is the way for the new generation. They almost expect it. The younger generation is even keener on it than the older ones in some ways. They are growing up to be more connected to their Māori heritage and want to use this as an opportunity for a wānanga or hui to help them connect with where they are from and show them the links between members of the whānau and the iwi.

Lately my boys have been coming home with homework from their Māori classes, wanting to know their maunga and so on for their mihi. The family meetings are great research opportunities for them. They understand even at their age that their whakapapa is so important. Understanding it together helps create a sense of purpose for us all.

They need to know where we've come from to see where we are going.

It's hard to give kids a consistent education in their culture. The eldest started at kōhanga reo and went onto kura kaupapa. Then when we moved he had to go to a mainstream school because there was no kura nearby. That was a hard decision because we really wanted our children to be totally immersed in te reo Māori. I was upset when that happened but we also saw that he had a good level of learning when he moved into mainstream, so that helped.

Somehow, with family functions and visits to Pawarenga and being around us, they have a good general knowledge of tikanga and marae protocol.

They know there is also a protocol here at the funeral home and behave accordingly. If there's a family here, they can't just

Mikae loves everything about tangi and funeral directing. When we lived upstairs at the funeral home, he would be downstairs pushing the caskets around on a trolley.

walk in and help themselves to the kitchen. They also know how to be useful. They will find more tissues and change the boxes if they are empty. The younger ones have got good at being quiet and just staying close to Mum and Dad until the families leave.

That is about as much as they can manage. When we visit the marae, they don't have the discipline or patience to sit inside and take in all the lessons. They want to be outside playing with their cousins. I wouldn't force them to sit there like our parents did.

Although that doesn't apply to Mikae. He would happily sit all day listening to waiata and kōrero and soaking it all up.

TWO WORKPLACES I think my older kids aren't that interested in going into are the funeral business or into television. Growing up with Tipene Funerals first and now *The Casketeers* in their lives has been a mixed experience for them. Nikora and Moronai have such big personalities of their own that they will only talk to people about *The Casketeers* if they are asked directly. As far as they are concerned, their mum and dad have jobs like everyone else's mum and dad have jobs. 'You going to work again, Dad? Okay, ka kite.'

The TV show has helped our younger children with their friends because they are able to watch it and know what Mikae and Mihaka's mum and dad do for a living and understand it, rather than thinking it is something weird.

Mikae and Mihaka love the funeral ceremony with all the prayers and singing. At home they play funeral directors, and one will be the dead body and the other one will push the casket. I guess if their parents were firefighters they would be running around screaming like sirens and pretending to put out fires.

Mikae loves everything about tangi and funeral directing. When we lived upstairs at the funeral home, he would be downstairs pushing the caskets around on a trolley and singing 'Whakaaria Mai' every chance he got.

Then we saw cracks and dings on one casket from all the shoving around, so we realised we didn't have a choice.

'You know what, son,' I said. 'You can have this casket if you want and you can do whatever with it.'

'I can have it?'

'Of course. Go for it.'

He would have been three going on four when that happened and he is still doing it now. He gets upset when we tell him he can't help us. Once when he wasn't allowed downstairs because there was a family there, he came upstairs and found a big storage bin, took the lid off, put his younger brother in and started singing 'Whakaaria Mai'.

He will grow out of it, but for now I think it is great that all the boys are comfortable with the business and just take it for granted. It is probably inevitable for the ones who spent years living above the funeral home.

I WORRY that the way we live our life may also have a downside for our children. Especially when I compare it to the way Kaiora and I were brought up.

I think we are spoiling them and letting them have things they don't need because we didn't get things when we were their age. I'm not really thinking about the effect it will have on them in the future.

The way I see it, they have been very patient with us. They got dragged along to work with us when they were small, and we put them to sleep in beds made up in our offices if we had to work into the night. I feel a bit bad looking back, but they were so young they don't remember much of it, if they remember anything at all. And they were fed, kept clean and able to sleep and be ready for school the next day. Hopefully they will remember that, whatever else happened, Mum and Dad were never far away. Now we want to make sure the children are supported in their desired areas of sport and their hobbies. And we do.

Our eldest boy, Nikora, needs the least. But when he does need something it will be a big-ticket item, like a laptop, which everyone has to have these days at school. But he is hardworking and grateful too. After school, he wanders down to the funeral home and asks if he can earn some money washing cars or doing something else useful. I love that attitude.

His attitude is different from ours. Because he has everything he wants, he doesn't worry so much about what he doesn't have. He can look at a shoe with a hole in it but won't want to part with it because it is his favourite.

It's good to see them developing interests that aren't just what we would like. Moronai loves car racing – especially V8s. He knows more about cars than I do. They are a passion he shares with my father. He will watch car racing on TV for hours at a time and wants to get into it himself.

It is a very expensive activity, but my wife and I are ready to support him if he really wants to do it. Like most parents of kids who are crazy about something, we face the dilemma of wanting to let him give it a go but not wanting to waste money if it doesn't work out. We might have a young champion in our family if we put the right energy in. Or we might not.

Our family is like all families – constantly changing and dealing together with the challenges kids face as they grow up.

We had one extra complication following the birth of Francis Jr. This time around the business was a bit busier than when the other boys had been born because of the TV. Work was through the roof for everyone. I promised my wife I'd have six months off to watch the baby and be a dad because I'd never been a hands-on dad with a baby before.

I didn't quite manage it, but I did take time off work, partly because Kaiora had to deal with post-natal depression (PND). For a long time, we thought she was just tired and would snap out of it, but it was much more serious than that. When we realised there was a name for what she was feeling, it was like a lightbulb being switched on. It's something she's confronted very bravely and, once again, it's better if she tells the story.

DARK DAYS

Kaiora: I was very surprised to be told I had post-natal depression. I was going through all these emotions after I had Francis Jr. I didn't expect anything unusual to happen. This was my fifth baby. And he was a good baby. He was behaving normally. Breastfeeding was going normally. I went home after the C-section and seemed to be recovering well.

But I was just exhausted. I was trying to get into a routine with my children and sort my husband out and I couldn't work out why it was so hard. I am a mum and used to being tired. I know how it is with a new baby.

But then Netflix happened. Francis Jr was still a new baby – about a week or two old – when the first series of our show was launched internationally and there was this completely unexpected global response.

The comments were lovely – so many from people who seemed to really appreciate what we were doing. I couldn't believe how much people liked it.

But in the middle of those comments there was other feedback: 'Oh, she's just the wife … She doesn't do much … She is just someone in the back seat.'

Nothing could be further from the truth, but out of the hundreds of positive comments, those few negative ones got me down. I'm unsure if they are what triggered my depression, but I know they didn't help.

Then season two came out in New Zealand. I had promotions to do for that. *Woman's Day* wanted to do things straight away, which was fair enough because we had signed a contract to do things to promote our show. But I wasn't feeling completely happy with my body. I certainly wasn't feeling like a glamorous TV star. I'd just had a baby and my stomach was all out of proportion. I wasn't looking how I wanted to look in photos.

And then something funny was happening to my heart. It wasn't working the way it should and I ended up in hospital on Christmas Eve. Mum was onto it straight away.

'Baby, are you okay?'

'I don't know, Mum. I'm alive.'

I managed to get to our Christmas Day lunch. Mum was looking at me very hard.

'Are you sure you're okay?'

Physically I was all right. I thought I was fine emotionally. But all these things must have been building up, because after I had baby Francis I found myself crying over whatever was happening at the time. It didn't matter what. Anything would set me off.

Then I became really ugly inside. I had negative energy consuming me and it was dragging in my husband, my children and the rest of my family. I didn't like that.

With my previous two babies, I just had them and kept going. Mikae came a month early but was just my normal C-section delivery. A week after the birth I was out of hospital and back at work with a baby in my arms because that was what I had to do. I was focused on building the business. When he was eight weeks old, we put him in daycare because he was waking up at night and staying awake during the day and I couldn't get any work done.

Eighteen months later, Mihaka came along. And it was the same again. Have him, go home, rest for a week, go back to work and take him along, and weeks later put him into daycare. And all that was fine at the time.

Then, when baby Francis came along, I couldn't feel the same way. It didn't feel like it would be normal to get straight back into things and bring him to work. There was some barrier stopping me from doing what I had done before.

It got worse. Around the time of New Year, when baby Francis was about three weeks old, I was crying, crying and crying. My husband would walk into the room and see my eyes puffed up and he didn't have a clue what was going on. Neither did I.

'Again, Kaiora? What's the problem now?'

I didn't know. I felt I was a burden to him. I rang my sister.

'What is going on?' she asked.

I tried to explain. 'Last night I got angry at my husband for not knowing how to make a bottle. Another time for not putting the right T-shirt on.'

It was only little things that got me depressed, but my husband triggered it. No matter what he did, any little thing would make me cry. Not the children. Or work. It was my husband.

'You tell me how your day goes tomorrow and we will talk tomorrow night,' said my sister.

And the next night when I reported in, my day had been just as bad. She recommended I go to the doctor, and I didn't react well to that.

'So now you think I'm crazy? I don't want to hear this. You're supposed to be supporting me.'

'I am truly helping you if anything.'

I suddenly felt I didn't need that kind of support. I felt judged, like I was doing something wrong when I couldn't help myself.

'This is quite serious,' she said. 'I'm trying to help you, and if you don't understand that, you should go to the doctor.'

I hung up. I didn't want to talk to her. There had been PND in my family before but none of us understood that at the time. We just thought my poor sister was being a pain.

I went to the doctor and pretty soon he confirmed PND. He recommended that I see a counsellor or at least make notes every day about what I was doing and how I was feeling.

And he told me I had to do something that was just for me – not for my husband, my baby or my business. That will be the start of something better. For the first time, I understood that depression was real and had to be taken seriously.

I did get some counselling but I kept putting off my appointment and only went twice. It felt weird just talking about myself. I know that's what you're supposed to do, but at the end of it I was expecting something to happen. I was waiting for him to tell me something. So I don't know if the strategy was healing me but when I left him I felt good. You should feel something for $160 an hour.

The Casketeers was another complication. Halfway through making season two we had been asked to do a third season. I was in the middle of my pregnancy and could barely see myself getting through season two, let alone think about committing to another one. I asked for some time to think about it and they were very understanding. They told me to take as long as I wanted and if I decided I couldn't commit to another series that would be fine.

But Francis was keen and I didn't want to be the one slowing everything down, so in the end I agreed. But when we were between seasons and the PND hit, I wanted to ask for a delay. I couldn't have gone ahead the way I was feeling.

The film crew were very understanding. This time we were able to shape the production around making more time for our kids and ourselves, and it was a much happier experience.

It was not as exhausting as the previous season was. It was even fun.

I only told a couple of my siblings about the PND, but when one knows anything they all do – there are females everywhere in my whānau. They tried to help. I got messages every day: 'How you going?' That was fine. But as the month went on, I felt it was just repetitive and didn't really change anything. 'We are here for you and we love you.' I felt like some lunatic who was supposed to call them, and I didn't like it.

'Can you not do that?' I said. 'I know you're there. I'm not suicidal just yet.'

But there were suicidal thoughts. It never got to the point where I was going to do anything, but it was a very dark and trying time mentally. There were moments when I felt life was pointless. If I'm always going to just exhaust myself in giving and giving and doing things and not getting anything in return or being acknowledged, then what was the point? Those are the feelings I was suffering with at the time.

I am happy that I didn't completely abandon Francis Jr, but I had those feelings too. Every so often I would think: *Life was fine before I had you.* The thought just popped into my head. I was resentful – all this exhaustion, all this punishment to my body for something that wasn't even making me happy.

Those thoughts came maybe every second day. It wasn't a constant feeling. I didn't just leave him in a room and let him cry. He wasn't responsible for how I felt. He was just part of something bigger that was going on in my head. In those dark moments, I would look at him and he would bring so much peace and joy that all of the mamae he had, he could also take away. He was part of my healing.

I did blame my husband a lot and felt I was unfair to him too, because I was making him unhappy. He was trying to help me deal with my unhappiness, and it became tiring for him. I didn't realise until later that he had taken a lot of time off work to help me and our family.

I wasn't behaving normally and he didn't know what to do. At one point, I just got in the car and drove for an hour to Waiuku without telling anyone. He called me.

'Where are you?' asked Francis.

'Why?'

'Because I'm allowed to know where you are.'

'No, you're not. You're not allowed to know where I am.'

'It's eight o'clock and I am at home. I just got in from today and you're not here. Don't you think that's weird?'

'Umm – well, did you think about how you spoke to me today?'

I changed it to make it a problem about something he had done. Eventually I just went home and that was that.

Now I can look back and appreciate that Francis was there and acknowledge that he did try to help. There were times he just wanted to give up too, but he stuck it out and is still tolerating me and I'm tolerating him. There's a lot of tolerating going on.

I think I still have a bit of depression. I'm not sure if it ever goes away altogether, but I'm a lot happier than before. I realise I had exhausted myself in giving, giving, giving to the point where I wasn't allowing myself anything.

I also went back to see another counsellor and that has made a huge difference.

My nights spent crying are getting fewer. Now if I cry it's usually because of another stupid thing Francis has purchased. I am accepting the way I feel a lot more. And when I take things out on Francis, he and I both know it is happening and can work with that.

There are still times in my day when something happens that upsets me and I start to focus on it in a dark way. But now I realise that is the depression. I'm working on it. I acknowledge those moments. I know that when they happen I need to get away from people and go into my own space. I lock myself in our office without Francis and deal with it. I have some deep breaths, tell myself to take it as a lesson and, when I am ready, I go back out again.

I hope it hasn't affected the children too much. They won't have many nice memories of Francis Jr's first few weeks. They saw me upset nearly every day in January and into February when I turned the corner. I was waking up upset every day and they knew it.

Eventually, Nikora spoke to my sister: 'My mum's been upset for a while. I don't know if it's my dad. It could be us, Aunty. I don't want to see my mum unhappy any more. I think she's telling us to go to Grandad's because she doesn't want us.'

That was upsetting to hear. I realised I needed to change things – and I have.

E kore e inaina ka pau te whakatau te hoe a Poupoto,
Tau ake ki te hoe a Kura e

———————————

Should the paddle of Poupoto struggle,
turn to the paddle of Kura

CHAPTER SEVENTEEN

PREPARE TO DIE

SOME PEOPLE are taken suddenly by death. Others know they are dying and have time to think about what it all means. Either way, it's a good idea to plan for your funeral in advance, and more and more people are doing this. When I started in the business, that was quite rare. People then weren't as ready to consider their own deaths as they are today. Now I get several people a week making appointments to discuss their arrangements.

But no matter how carefully you plan, the fact is when it is time to put that plan in action, you won't be around to make it happen. When you are dead, it is those left behind who make the decision. And funerals are for the living.

Some people come in and tell me in great detail about the funeral they want, complete with the readings and the music and what kind of flowers. But it is all hypothetical and maybe years in the future. Some people may be telling me this in order to sidestep their families because they don't trust them to do what they would want.

If a person is terminally ill, they shouldn't be burdened with lots of questions. 'Where do you want to be buried? Is it okay for your ex-wife to come? Who do you not want at the funeral?'

Which is why my biggest piece of advice to people is to talk to their families about their wishes. The more people who know what you would like, the better. But instead, people often come to me to have a secret chat.

'Francis, I have some very specific instructions for how I want things done.'

'Fine, but have you told your family? You need them onside. It may not be what they would want.'

Then we end up getting into some deep conversations.

Some come in knowing what they want but ready to consider other options. Then we talk about costs, choosing between cremation or burial, what type of viewing or service they would like. If any. A lot of people are choosing not to have any kind of service.

Many people are motivated by a desire to spare their family trouble and expense. They worry that their loved ones will be shelling out thousands on flowers and food. We funeral directors have shot ourselves in the foot by making the options for funerals so elaborate that we have scared people off.

A lot of people are saying they don't want to be viewed: 'Just close me up and take me to the crematorium.' And there have always been those people who say they don't want a fancy coffin: 'Just put me in a cardboard box.' Which is fine, but even then, a cardboard box will be $250.

This discussion is an opportunity to let them know not only how they can affect the funeral but also how their choices will affect the people who are left. It's good if the whole family can discuss this because it has an impact on them. Grandma might say she wants to be taken from the hospice to the crematorium with no one present and have the ashes sent to the grandchildren. But I will point out that there is an emotional cost if the family haven't had the chance to take part in the farewell.

A lot of people say it's a sales tactic to sell coffins and cupcakes. A lot of other people end up regretting that they never got to see their mother when she was dead and that they think about it every day.

If we give people even ten or fifteen minutes to see Grandma in the casket, to understand she is dead and to say farewell, it's going to help them in the long run. Grandma doesn't need to be embalmed. All that's needed is a little ceremony, a gathering of people whose lives she was part of, some karakia and a waiata. All those things are very low cost but together they have a big impact.

Lives have a beginning, middle and end, and each stage needs to be marked as a new chapter, including the last one.

People worry about children around dead bodies, but children are resilient. They often handle death better than adults do, probably because they haven't had a lifetime of worrying about it. It's healthy for them to see Grandma in her casket so that they understand how final death is. They don't need protecting from it.

I think there is nothing worse than a closed casket at a funeral. Everyone knows Grandma is in there, but subconsciously there is always this weird niggle: *Is she really? How do we know Francis hasn't put something else in there he wants to get rid of?*

Of course, it's better to say goodbye before the person dies. You get the chance to tell Grandma how much you love her, and she will be able to tell you how much she loves you.

People don't realise it, but in cases of terminal diagnoses, they have effectively started the funeral while the person is still alive. This is very healing in the days after the death itself.

I know because people often bring it up in eulogies if they have been able to visit the loved one in the hospital or hospice. 'I am so glad I got to say this, to see you, to have this moment, and the last thing you said to me was this ...' For a lot of people, it's about having had that time.

Hopefully, visitors to people who are dying will concentrate on the important things. If a person is terminally ill, they shouldn't be burdened with lots of questions. 'Where do you want to be buried? Is it okay for your ex-wife to come? Who do you not want at the funeral? What sort of casket do you want? What colour coffin?'

In the end, the person is dead and gone, and there will still be grief, no matter how much time you have had to prepare, but there are degrees of grief.

This is why sudden deaths are so sad. People haven't had a chance to get used to the fact that Grandma won't be around any more, let alone to say goodbye to her. In those cases, I look for ways to support the whānau.

People still attend funerals if death hasn't been sudden, but they won't make it a mission to get there because being with a person when they are dying and having some true bonding time is more healing than attending the funeral. That is evident with the numbers you get at the different kinds of funerals.

Sudden death funerals are always going to be big. People didn't get to say goodbye before Grandma died so they will be determined to get to her farewell. Funerals where people have been ill for a long time are often smaller.

In a sudden death – Grandma is just gone. The last thing you might have said to Grandma might have been something angry or thoughtless, and this makes the blow harder. Turning up to her funeral balances that a little by letting you show respect.

Shock galvanises people. There is usually one person who is the backbone of the family and steps up to take charge of everything and pull everyone together. They probably do this for other family events too.

Māori and Pacific Island families go all out in these cases, especially when it comes to financial assistance. They will go without, sometimes to their own detriment, to help others. It's a beautiful thing to see the community rallying around to support people who might be in a state of shock.

Then there are people who know they are dying, have accepted their terminal diagnosis and come in to make their own arrangements. They are not dead, of course, but they are not really alive either – they are actually in the process of dying.

There have been cases where I had a full-on conversation about their death with a person who seemed to be as healthy as me or anyone I know. I listen politely and am thinking: *Look at you. There is no way you are dying.*

And two or three weeks later, they have passed away. They had no life expectancy on their part.

I find that a little bit freaky. I have made a connection with a living person sitting up in our lounge, and here they are back again to be prepared, embalmed and dressed.

With a kuia or an elderly person, it is one thing. I'm pretty good at handling that. But when they are only in their forties or fifties, I struggle. I think: *Did I treat them nicely? Did I give them enough attention?*

*

IT'S NOT UNUSUAL for a family member to come in when their relative is in the last stages of an illness. But it is unusual for them to name the day the funeral will be.

One morning I was having my hair cut up the road and the gentleman in the next chair recognised me from *The Casketeers*.

'Oh my gosh, it's Francis Tipene,' he said. 'I'm just coming to see you.'

'Really?'

'Yes – I've come to get a haircut first. But you are here. I'm coming down to your building.'

'Neat. I look forward to seeing you there.'

'My mum is on her way out.'

'Oh, I'm sorry. Well, I'll see you soon.'

And a couple of minutes after I got back to work, he walked in with his brother and we all sat down to kōrero.

'Our mum's not doing well, so we are trying to organise her funeral and hoping for Friday.'

'Where is Mum?'

'Auckland Hospital.'

'Is Mum alive?'

'Oh yeah, Mum is still alive, but we want to plan her funeral for Friday.'

It was Tuesday. I had a laugh to myself. Then I said, 'Obviously, this is all in God's hands,' but they didn't seem very worried about my reservations.

'Oh yeah, we know that. We'd like a family service on Thursday and the funeral on Friday. We want to keep to Mum's wishes.'

We went through all the details. The gentleman was very organised and followed his mum's wishes to the letter.

There are often arguments when someone leaves instructions to one child and doesn't tell the others. You get a real kerfuffle. Or, I should say, I get a real kerfuffle.

Fortunately, she had left instructions to all three of her sons. That made it so beautiful because they were all on the same page. There are often arguments when someone leaves instructions to one child and doesn't tell the others. You get a real kerfuffle. Or, I should say, I get a real kerfuffle, because the funeral director is the one caught in the middle waiting for everyone to agree.

This was a Samoan family and the only challenge brought up by the mother's instructions was that she wanted her funeral over and done with quickly. Customarily, a Samoan funeral will take at least three days and as many as five or six. They can be quite drawn out, so she was going against tradition in that respect.

Lo and behold, on Tuesday night she died.

As requested, we had a family service on Thursday and buried her on Friday.

Of course, at the family service this sequence of events was all anyone talked about. Everyone could not believe the story when it was shared. 'Mum, it has all worked out as you wanted it.'

The other funny thing was that her whole life had been about timing. She worked at Auckland Hospital for many years and she loved punctuality.

It all fell into place because she organised it and spoke to her children.

My advice to everyone – whether they are sick or not, whether they think Mum is going to die on Tuesday night or not – is to have the conversation and talk to as many family members as possible with the same story to save problems.

People get hung up on wills and getting other documents written up, and they are important for disposal of assets and bequests and other things that are left behind. But when it comes to people – who are the most important things of all – and your funeral, they are not part of the story.

When people leave no hint about what they want, it gets very complicated, and a lot will depend on the dynamics within the family. In some groups, we see a fair bit of power tripping: 'Mum is dead and I am the eldest so I am the head of the family now.' And if there is one family member who is better off and likely to be shouldering the financial burden, they are likely to throw their weight around.

That's sad. Funerals are for the living, but they're not for the living to show who is top dog.

This can happen in Māori families. According to the strict interpretation of tikanga, it is the right way. But it's better if everyone can agree together on things. In te reo Māori, we say 'Kua ngū' – he is silent. That might sound a bit harsh, but it just means it is up to the living to speak.

Finally, be like the Tipene whānau and put some money away to pay for the funeral so that there won't be a burden left for the family. I like to be paid. So do other funeral homes. There are external costs that we take care of: catering, flowers, service sheets, celebrants. The funeral home disburses all these fees before we get any ourselves. We can suddenly have thousands of dollars in debt that is not actually ours. Multiply that by a few funerals a week and we risk real financial trouble.

This is why we never try to upsell. It is not worth the risk of somebody not being able to pay for the beautiful casket we have encouraged them to buy.

I wish everyone could afford a beautiful custom-made casket, but they can't. I probably don't help with the way I display the caskets and polish them all the time. I keep them so shiny and glamorous and beautiful, you can't help but want to buy one.

We try to get everyone to take the most affordable option for their circumstances. We have to give people the account and if it is a lot of money, we get whakamā. There is a fine line between care and love and aroha on the one hand and a huge account to pay for it all on the other. It's not about the casket, it is about who is in the casket.

I whiria ai te mate
hei taura kumekume i a tāua ki te pō e

———————————

Death has been woven into a cord
that draws us into the great night

CHAPTER EIGHTEEN

AND WHEN I DIE

LIKE EVERYTHING ELSE in life, death changes with the times. Funerals are adjusting to the twenty-first century and there are some debates in Māoridom over what should happen when new technology comes up against the old ways. I think they can get along just fine.

Many funerals are livestreamed now. It's basic technology available to most people. Everyone has it on their smartphone, or the smartphone of the person sitting next to them.

I think livestreaming is in keeping with Māori tradition. It allows us to capture the beautiful kōrero that is heard at a tangi, archive it and keep it for future generations. That has to be a good thing. And it is the way we have always worked because Māori teaching was transmitted orally – just like when my Uncle Nick told me about the early funerals at Pawarenga.

You will often hear Māori say, 'My tūpuna said …' or 'Nana said …' A lot of those things still aren't written down.

But if we can keep visual and aural documentation, showing why and how we did things, there is a lot of learning that will be kept forever. The learning is fluid because the knowledge changes. When you write something down, you tend to think it is fixed and there is no progress.

But when something is livestreamed – whether it is at a tangi or a hui or anything else – it is like a whare wānanga. I find it very moving. I am a big advocate for getting internet access extended to our remotest marae because of its power to bring everyone together.

And Māori being such a poetic language, it is meant to be heard, so you can appreciate the music of it. It loses a lot when it is just lying there on the page.

So I am all for livestreaming of tangi. It is done a lot in Pacific Island and Pākehā communities as well. At cemeteries, people always want to know what the link to the service is so they can pass it on to those who can't attend and record it themselves to keep as a memento.

I have noticed that when a Pākehā funeral is livestreamed, about 60 per cent more people tune in than do so for a Māori or Pacific Island one. We get the statistics from the services at the end of the month and I can always tell just from the numbers whether or not it was a Pākehā funeral.

I know livestreaming means fewer people will go to a funeral. As things get more expensive and people want to reduce the amount they travel, those are things we have to deal with. But although there might not be as many people there in person, there will be more people attending overall because they can do it via Skype or Facetime. It's a great solution for those people who can't get back from overseas in time or get away from work for three days to tangi for their family.

Being Māori, of course, we are having major debates among ourselves about these changes. We need to sit down in our iwi and have a big kōrero to decide what we think about these issues. How far are we willing to go to change our tikanga or funeral practices, with this livestreaming? Personally, I would love to have webcams all over the marae so we can see what we are doing.

But there are issues with livestreaming. Issues about tangi when only five people bother to go in person. Issues about privacy if people don't want to be seen in the midst of their grief. Issues about respect and how much of the body itself we would be willing to show in this way. Issues about the younger generation being even further removed from their tikanga because they are not taking part directly but just treating it like another video game.

As a culture we are communal people, with everything done together. We don't feel right making decisions without running them past everyone. Even at Tipene Funerals – sometimes to my detriment – I run things past not only my wife but staff as well. I have to make sure everyone's on board, because we all have to do it together.

I think *The Casketeers* has helped pave the way for change because it has got people used to seeing tangi and even parts of the body itself on TV.

Hopefully, funerals won't end up like sports events – with no one bothering to go but just staying home and watching it on TV. That would be very sad because we would miss the sense of community and aroha and all the great things that come out of getting together and interacting with other people – like the things that happened at Pop's unveiling.

Being present is an important part of tangi tradition. There's a beautiful old te reo Māori phrase that a lot of people say when they turn up to funerals: 'They told me you were dead but I've come to see your face so I know for myself.' And they will have quite a conversation with the dead person: 'I've come all the way here from Auckland … I got a phone call and they said you had passed away, but I said I would not believe it unless I saw it with my own eyes.' On a livestream, you can still see someone is dead, but it's not quite the same.

Technology has made our work within the company more efficient too. Some of the big firms have fantastic systems. There is great software that looks after everything on an iPad from the moment a funeral comes in. The details are entered and it is all there on the screen for everyone in the company to see. They know who the person is, they know who is going to be doing the funeral and where and when, and all the other parts of the arrangement are there so the chances of something going wrong are reduced.

Not so long ago it was blackboards and chalk or whiteboards and Vivids to keep track of the work. This is a lot more efficient.

I would love all our staff to have an iPad, but they are expensive. If I want one for everyone in the firm, I'm going to have to think about how much we will grow. Although it's not quite the same, we do have a Facebook page for staff, where we note what we are doing and hopefully everyone else sees it.

Kaiora and I aren't sure how big we want the business to get. We have a daydream of going back to being the little funeral firm we used to be. In some ways, we may have been happier then. Things were more intimate. We didn't have all those kids or staff.

'I've come all the way here from Auckland … I got a phone call and they said you had passed away, but I said I would not believe it unless I saw it with my own eyes.'

We love all our staff. They really are like another whānau. We don't want to let them down. We know they have bills to pay and love their jobs, but every minute we spend with them is a minute we're not spending with each other. We used to like spending more time working together.

There are a couple of small companies out there I am envious of – a husband and wife doing two to six funerals a month. That won't make you rich, but it's manageable. I never wanted to be rich, and I still don't. But in order to downsize we'd have to turn a lot of work away and I know that would be disappointing people, even though it might be good for our stress levels.

We already have many more demands on our time than we used to, partly because of *The Casketeers* and the interest that has raised, but also because of the size of the firm.

I know I'm supposed to think of the big picture because that is what good business people do. But I can't. There is no big picture. There is no long-term plan. There is no 'Where do we see ourselves in five years?'

Of course, we'd like to own our own home. We're like any other couple our age in that respect. Now Pop's big unveiling is over, we can concentrate on saving. That's as far as we have thought. I don't even know if we want to buy a home or build our own. We just want somewhere we can say is our little bit, where the boys can have some space to grow up in and that we can call home.

At the moment, everything goes into the business. When I am doing funerals, I am always thinking about them from a business point of view. I ask myself how the business is ticking over commercially – but, also, pulling in the opposite direction, I'm asking how I can help each family make their loved one's funeral memorable with what money they have.

The bigger we get, the less of a funeral director I am, because I have to pull back on doing funerals in order to be a manager.

The hard part is knowing when to stop. The bigger we get, the closer we get to having to hand over to a professional manager and let other people do things that we can still do all by ourselves. It won't be the same then.

Kaiora probably thinks more about goals than I do. I am very conscious that I am young and inexperienced when it comes to the business side of running a business. Kaiora runs it, not me. She is the businessperson in the family. I'm not a businessperson. I'm just good at my job. But, to be honest, we wouldn't be where we are today if it wasn't for her. And it's obvious that I wouldn't want it any other way. I need to acknowledge my wife more often. I am grateful for everything she does. She is my wife, the mother to my children and then my business partner. She is my rock and I love doing life with her.

AND WHEN I DIE I have a few ideas of my own for what I would like to happen. Kaiora and I will probably end up on the land at Pawarenga in some form or other. But my personal ideal funeral isn't like the ones I do for other people.

For instance, if my wife or I died, I'd like to have a bit of one of our bones cut out and carved and made into a beautiful taonga that could be kept in the family for generations. That was done in the old days with prominent people. It's illegal now, but I've always thought it would be good to do.

The main thing about bones back then was to keep them hidden from the enemy while the flesh was decaying on them during hahunga. They had to be very well concealed because it was the ultimate insult to desecrate your enemy's bones. If you did that, you had won the final victory.

I'd like a version of the hahunga practice too. I'd like to be put in the open air, especially being a claustrophobic person. I do have a real fear of being buried alive, even though I know that could never happen.

I'd love to be put into some sort of natural mausoleum – like a tree – where nature could take its course with my body. When scavengers eat remains, that is just nature going around in its great cycle. I like the idea of being part of that. Then those bones could be taken and given to my mokopuna for carving or preserving.

But I think what will actually happen is that my wife and I will be put in a mausoleum together to wait for the Second Coming. That is the destiny our Mormon faith promises us. I also like that with a mausoleum there is a key, and people can come and visit whenever they want. We would be in zinc-lined, solid wood caskets, sitting – or lying – there on a shelf where people could easily come and say hello.

GLOSSARY

ao	world
aroha	love; sympathy; compassion
haere mai	come hither
haere rā	farewell (to someone who is leaving)
hahunga	ceremony for uplifting bones
haka	dance; performance
hapū	pregnant; kinship group
hīmene	hymn
hōhā	annoying
hongi	greeting by pressing noses together
hua	prick
hui	meeting
iwi	tribe
ka kite (anō)	see you later
ka pai	good
kai	food; eat
kaiako	teacher
kāinga	home
kapa haka	Māori performing arts; performing group
karakia	prayer
karanga	welcome call

kaumātua	elder
kaupapa	mission
kawa	marae protocol
kawe mate	mourning ceremony for a deceased person after their funeral has been completed and their remains laid to rest
kia ora	hello; thank you
koha	donation; gift
kōhanga reo	Māori language pre-school
kōkōwai	red ochre
kōrero	talk; narrative
kuia	elderly woman
kura kaupapa	Māori language immersion school
mahi	work
mamae	pain
mana	prestige; status
manaakitanga	hospitality
manuhiri	visitors
Māoritanga	Māori way of life
marae	meeting house grounds
mate	death; dying
matua	elder; senior male
maunga	mountain
mihi	greet(ing)
mokopuna	grandchild(ren)
noa	common; unrestricted; ordinary
Pākehā	non-Māori
pēpi	baby
pō	darkness

pou	pole; expert
pōwhiri	welcoming ceremony
puku	stomach
rangatira	chief; important
raruraru	conflict
reo	language
tamariki	children
tangi	funeral; cry; wail
tangihanga	funeral
taonga	treasure
tapu	sacred; set apart
taumata	summit
tautoko	support
tikanga	protocol
tohunga	priest; expert
tono	request
tukutuku	decorative lattice-work
tūpāpaku	body of the deceased
tūpuna	ancestors
tūrangawaewae	place of belonging
urupā	cemetery
wāhi tapu	sacred place; burial ground
waiata	song; sing
wairua	spirit
wānanga	tertiary institution; shared learning and discussion
whaea	senior woman
whaikōrero	formal speeches
whakamā	embarrassed; shy

whakapapa	genealogy
'Whakaaria Mai'	'How Great Thou Art' (hymn)
whānau	family; to birth
whāngai	feed; Māori custom of fostering children
whare	house; building
wharekai	dining hall
wharenui	meeting house
whenua	land; placenta